INTELLIGENT MACHINES: UNDERSTANDING THE RISE OF ARTIFICIAL INTELLIGENCE

ISHWARYA M V

Made with ♥ on the Notion Press Platform
www.notionpress.com

Contents

1. Introduction   1

2. Programming With Ai   19

3. Research Areas Of ai   30

4. Reinforcement Learning   73

5. Ai Revolution   112

CHAPTER ONE

Introduction

How can artificial intelligence be defined?

Artificial intelligence (AI) is the capacity for thought and learning in a computer programme or other system. It has been characterised in a variety of ways, but generally speaking, it can be regarded as a method of making a computer system "smart," or able to comprehend and follow complex directions.

A subfield of computer science called artificial intelligence is concerned with building intelligent machines that function and respond much like people.

Artificial intelligence (AI) is the capacity for thought and learning in a computer programme or other system. The development of intelligent machines that function and respond just like people is the focus of this area of computer science.

The History of AI :

AI is a field of computer science that focuses on creating intelligent machines that can work and react like humans. It has been around since the 1950s, but has seen a lot of growth in recent years. AI is used in a variety of fields, including robotics, natural language processing, computer vision, and machine learning.

The history of AI can be traced back to the early 1950s, when British computer scientist Alan Turing proposed the idea of a "Turing Test" for determining a machine's ability to "think" like a human. The test involves having a human and a machine answer questions and determine which one is the human. While Turing's test was never used in practice, it inspired the field of AI.

In the 1950s, scientists began to explore how to teach machines to think and act like humans. This led to the development of AI programming languages, such as LISP and Prolog. In the 1960s, AI began to be used in a variety of applications, such as robotics and natural language processing.

In the 1970s, AI made a major breakthrough with the development of expert systems. These are computer programs that are designed to solve problems by making decisions based on its knowledge of a particular domain. Expert systems were used in a variety of industries, including medicine, finance, and engineering.

In the 1980s, AI saw a further increase in popularity as researchers began to explore the potential of machine learning. This is a subfield of AI that focuses on using algorithms to teach machines how to learn from data. This led to the development of neural networks, which are used to model complex relationships between input and output data.

In the 1990s, AI saw a major breakthrough with the development of deep learning. This is a more advanced form of machine learning that uses layers of artificial "neurons" to identify patterns in data. This has enabled AI to be used in a variety of applications, such as image recognition, natural language processing, and autonomous vehicles.

Artificial Intelligence (AI) has been around since the 1950s. The term was first coined in 1956 by John McCarthy, a computer scientist at Dartmouth College. AI began with a series of conferences and workshops that aimed to explore how computers could be used to simulate human intelligence. Early work in AI focused on problem solving and game playing, and in the 1970s AI began to make significant progress in robotics and natural language processing. In the 1980s, AI research shifted to the application of expert systems, which are computer programs designed to mimic the decision-making process of a human expert.

In the early 1990s, AI experienced a resurgence with the development of machine learning and neural networks, which are computer algorithms that can learn from data and recognize patterns. This led to the development of intelligent agents and autonomous robots. AI has since been used in a variety of applications, including medical diagnosis, self-driving cars, facial recognition, and natural language processing. AI is continuously evolving and is being used to solve increasingly complex problems.

Today, AI is used in a wide variety of fields, including healthcare, finance, and transportation. It is also used in consumer products, such as virtual assistants and smart home devices. AI is continuing to evolve, with researchers exploring new ways to use machine learning and deep learning to create smarter and more efficient machines.

The First Beginnings :

The first experiments in artificial intelligence began in the 1950s. Early researchers in the field of AI sought to develop machines that could solve problems and make decisions with minimal human intervention. Through a combination of computer programming, machine learning, and natural language processing, researchers developed algorithms that could recognize patterns and respond to stimuli in a more intelligent way.

One of the key early breakthroughs in AI was the development of the perceptron algorithm, developed by Frank Rosenblatt in 1957. The algorithm allowed computers to recognize patterns in data, and it formed the basis for many of the early AI applications.

In the 1960s, AI researchers began to explore the possibility of machine learning, which involved creating computer programs that could learn from data and make decisions without relying on explicit programming. Researchers also began to explore topics such as natural language processing, which enabled computers to understand human language.

In the 1970s, AI research focused on developing computer vision and robotics, in order to create machines that could interact with their environment. In addition, AI researchers began to explore the idea of expert systems, which allowed computers to emulate the behavior of experts in a particular field.

Since then, AI research has expanded to encompass a wide range of disciplines and applications, including machine learning, natural language processing, robotics, computer vision, and more. The field of AI has rapidly evolved over the last few decades, and it continues to be a major focus of research in computer science.

Logic Solves (Almost) All Problems :

Logic is a powerful tool when it comes to solving problems in AI. It can be used to represent a problem in a way that can be understood by computers, and it can be used to determine the best possible solution to a given problem.

Logic can also be used to create rules, which can help an AI system to better understand and respond to certain situations. Finally, logic can be used to create algorithms that can help an AI system to more efficiently find a solution to a given problem.

Logic can be used in AI to solve problems in a variety of ways. For example, it can be used to identify patterns and relationships between data points. This can help AI systems determine which actions will be most effective in achieving a goal. Logic can also be used to develop algorithms that can identify and classify objects, as well as recognize and respond to natural language.

Logic is an invaluable tool for solving many problems. While it can't solve all problems, it can help to break down complex issues and provide a structured approach to help find solutions. Logic can be used to identify patterns, create hypotheses, and evaluate evidence. It can also be used to make decisions and develop strategies. Logic is an essential skill used by scientists, engineers, lawyers, and many other professionals to solve problems and make decisions.

Logic is an important tool for solving problems. In fact, it is arguably the most important tool for problem solving. Logic allows us to analyze and break down a problem into its components, identify the relationships between them, and then determine the best solution. Logic can be used to create algorithms, which are step-by-step instructions for solving a problem. Algorithms, in turn, can be used to create computer programs that solve a problem efficiently and reliably. Logic can also be used to reason about the properties of systems and to make predictions about their behavior. Thus, logic is a powerful tool for solving a wide variety of problems.

In addition to its applications in problem-solving, logic can also be used to automate the process of learning. By using logical rules, machines can determine which data points are important and which can be ignored. This can help AI systems learn from experience and improve their understanding of a given task or environment.

Logic is an important tool for AI because it allows machines to make decisions based on rational thought. It helps them to think more like humans and better understand the world. While logic does not solve all problems in AI, it is a powerful tool for making AI systems smarter and more capable.

Philosophy of AI :

The philosophy of AI is the branch of philosophy that deals with questions and concerns related to the development and use of artificial intelligence. It seeks to understand the ethical implications of AI, as well as its impact on society, the economy, and the environment. It also explores the philosophical implications of AI, such as whether AI can be conscious, and if so, what are the implications of that consciousness? Additionally, the philosophy of AI examines the ethical implications of using AI for decision-making, such as in the case of autonomous vehicles. Finally, it also seeks to understand the implications of AI on the future of work, as well as the implications of AI in areas such as healthcare, military, and education.

The philosophy of AI is the study of how intelligent machines, such as computers, can be used to help us think and make decisions, and how their use affects our lives. It is an interdisciplinary field that combines philosophy, computer science, artificial intelligence, and cognitive science.

The philosophy of AI is concerned with understanding the nature and implications of artificial intelligence. It examines the potential of AI to enable machines to think, reason, learn, and act autonomously, as well as its potential implications for humanity. Key topics include understanding what AI is, the implications of current and near-future AI technologies, the ethical and legal implications of AI, and the potential for AI to benefit or harm humanity. Ultimately, the philosophy of AI seeks to answer questions about the nature of intelligence, the implications of AI, and the potential for AI to shape the future of humanity.

The philosophy of AI is concerned with understanding how intelligent machines can be created and how they interact with their environment. It is also concerned with understanding how to use AI responsibly and ethically. The philosophy of AI is an interdisciplinary field, drawing on ideas from philosophy, computer science, psychology, and neuroscience. It explores topics such as artificial general intelligence, machine learning, robotics, and autonomous systems. It also examines the implications of AI on society, and the ethical and moral consequences of its use.

The philosophy of AI is the branch of philosophy that studies the nature of artificial intelligence and its implications for how we think about the world. It is a branch of philosophy that seeks to understand the implications of AI on human life and its relationship to ethical and moral considerations. AI is increasingly being used in a wide range of areas, from healthcare to transportation, and its implications for the future of humanity are profound. AI has the potential to impact our lives in dramatic and unpredictable ways, and the philosophy of AI seeks to explore the implications of this technology for humanity and its future.

The philosophy of AI is the branch of philosophy that studies the nature of artificial intelligence and its implications for how we think about the world. It is a branch of philosophy that seeks to understand the implications of AI on human life and its relationship to ethical and moral considerations. AI is increasingly being used in a wide range of areas, from healthcare to transportation, and its implications for the future of humanity are profound. AI has the potential to impact our lives in dramatic and unpredictable ways, and the philosophy of AI seeks to explore the implications of this technology for humanity and its future.

Goals of AI:

1. Automating Intelligent Behaviors: Creating intelligent machines and software that can interact with their environment and make decisions with minimal human intervention.
2. Problem Solving: Developing machines and software that can solve problems in a wide range of fields, such as logistics, medical diagnosis, and robotics.
3. Knowledge Representation: Creating machines and software that can learn from experience and store and manipulate large amounts of data.
4. Natural Language Processing: Developing machines and software that can understand, interpret, and generate natural language.
5. Computer Vision: Developing machines and software that can recognize and interpret visual information.

6. Robotics: Creating robots that can sense, plan, and act autonomously.

The goals of AI generally include:
1. Automating processes for greater efficiency and accuracy
2. Improving decision-making and problem-solving
3. Creating intelligent systems that can interact with humans
4. Detecting patterns and anomalies in data
5. Developing models and simulations to predict outcomes
6. Creating autonomous robots and vehicles
7. Developing natural language processing and voice recognition capabilities
8. Enhancing conversations between humans and machines
9. Creating autonomous agents that can interact with humans
10. Enhancing the security of digital systems and networks

The main goals of AI are to:
1. Create intelligent machines that can think, learn, and act like humans.
2. Develop machines that can perceive their environment and act accordingly.
3. Automate repetitive tasks with minimal human intervention.
4. Create machines that can understand natural language and interact with humans.
5. Develop machines that can solve complex problems and make decisions.

6. Create machines that can recognize patterns, detect anomalies, and make predictions.

7. Enable machines to learn from their mistakes and improve over time.

8. Develop machines that can act autonomously and collaboratively with humans.

What Contributes to AI?

AI is comprised of several different elements, including but not limited to the following:

1. Machine Learning: Machine learning is a subfield of computer science that focuses on giving computers the ability to learn from data without explicit programming. Machine learning algorithms can be used to analyze large amounts of data, identify patterns, and make predictions and decisions.

2. Natural Language Processing: Natural language processing (NLP) is a subfield of artificial intelligence that focuses on giving computers the ability to understand and interpret natural language.

3. Computer Vision: Computer vision is a subfield of artificial intelligence that focuses on giving computers the ability to recognize objects and interpret visual data.

4. Robotics: Robotics is a subfield of artificial intelligence that focuses on giving machines the ability to autonomously complete tasks.

5. Knowledge Representation and Reasoning: Knowledge representation and reasoning is a subfield of artificial intelligence that focuses on giving computers the ability to understand complex relationships and use them to make decisions.

AI is made up of many different components and technologies, including machine learning, natural language processing, robotics, computer vision, and artificial neural networks. These technologies are used to create systems that can learn, reason, and act autonomously. AI can also be used to develop algorithms that can be used to make decisions or predictions. Additionally, AI can be used to automate tasks and processes, as well as provide insights into data and trends.

AI is a broad field that encompasses many different disciplines, including computer science, mathematics, linguistics, robotics, neuroscience, philosophy, and psychology. It involves the use of algorithms, data structures, and artificial intelligence to solve complex problems. AI also utilizes machine learning and deep learning techniques, which allow machines to learn from data and make decisions without human intervention. AI systems can be used to automate mundane tasks, automate decision-making processes, understand natural language, and provide insights into complex data sets. AI is being used in many different industries, including healthcare, finance, retail, transportation, and customer service.

AI is created through a combination of various different technologies, including machine learning algorithms, data mining, and natural language processing. AI also relies heavily on access to large amounts of data, which allows it to learn and improve its performance. Additionally, AI relies heavily on computing power and resources, as it requires huge amounts of data and computing power to process and analyze all of the data it collects. Finally, AI also relies on advances in hardware and software engineering to create faster and more efficient algorithms.

AI is made up of several components, including:

1. Machine Learning: Machine learning is the process by which machines are able to learn from data and make decisions without being explicitly programmed.

2. Natural Language Processing: Natural language processing (NLP) is a subfield of artificial intelligence that focuses on understanding how computers can interpret and interact with human language.

3. Computer Vision: Computer vision is a branch of artificial intelligence that enables machines to interpret and understand visual data from images and videos.

4. Robotics: Robotics is an interdisciplinary branch of engineering and science that deals with the design, construction, operation, and application of robots.

5. Neural Networks: Neural networks are computer systems modeled after the human brain that are capable of learning from data.

6. Knowledge Representation: Knowledge representation is the process of representing knowledge in a format that can be understood by a machine.

7. Automation: Automation is the use of computer systems to perform tasks that would otherwise be done by humans.

8. Planning & Scheduling: Planning and scheduling are techniques used to optimize processes and operations.

Programming Without and With AI :

Programming Without AI:

Programming without AI typically involves using code to create algorithms that can accomplish certain tasks. This could include creating a web page, writing a game, or creating a program to calculate something. This type of programming typically requires a programmer to have a good understanding of the language they are coding in and a clear understanding of the problem they are trying to solve.

Programming without AI involves writing code using programming languages such as C, C++, Java, HTML, CSS, and JavaScript. Programming without AI involves writing code to create applications, websites, and software programs without using AI techniques such as machine learning, natural language processing, and deep learning. Examples of programming without AI include creating websites, web applications, desktop applications, mobile applications, and games. Programming without AI also involves writing code to control robotic systems, embedded systems, and the Internet of Things (IoT).

Programming without AI is still possible using traditional programming languages such as C, C++, Java, and Python. These languages can be used to create applications, websites, databases, and other software without the use of AI algorithms. While AI can greatly enhance the capabilities of certain applications, it is not necessary in all cases.

Programming without AI can involve coding applications or websites, building databases, creating algorithms, and much more. Depending on the type of programming being done, the developer may use different languages, such as HTML, CSS, JavaScript, SQL, PHP, and more. They may also use different frameworks and libraries to help them create the programs. Additionally, they may have to use tools such as source control, debugging, and testing tools.

Brain Science and Problem Solving :

The field of artificial intelligence (AI) has seen tremendous growth in recent years, as advances in neuroscience and computing power have allowed for the development of increasingly powerful AI systems. One important application of AI is in the area of problem solving, which involves the use of a variety of techniques to identify and solve complex problems.

Neuroscience has played an important role in the development of AI problem-solving techniques. Neuroscientists have studied the brain's role in problem solving, and have identified various patterns of neural activity associated with successful problem solving. This has allowed AI researchers to develop algorithms that can mimic the same patterns of neural activity, enabling AI systems to tackle complex problems more effectively.

Problem solving is an essential part of the brain's functioning. By understanding how the brain works, we can learn to be more effective problem solvers. Brain science helps us understand the cognitive processes involved in problem solving, such as attention, working memory, decision-making, and planning. It also reveals the physical networks that are activated during problem solving, such as the prefrontal cortex, hippocampus, and other brain regions associated with executive functioning.

In addition, research on the brain's reward system can help us identify incentives and rewards that motivate us to solve problems. Finally, understanding the neuroscience of emotion can help us recognize when we are feeling overwhelmed or discouraged and how to respond to these feelings in a way that helps us stay focused and productive. With a better understanding of how the brain works, we can develop better problem-solving strategies and become more successful in our endeavors.

In addition, neuroscience has provided insight into the types of problems that are best suited to AI-based solutions. By understanding the biological basis of problem-solving behavior, AI researchers are better equipped to create algorithms that can efficiently and accurately solve problems.

Finally, neuroscience has also provided insight into the potential applications of AI in the real world. By understanding the neurological basis of decision making, AI can be used to automate or optimize tasks that involve making decisions. This has a wide range of potential applications, from medical diagnosis to financial trading.

The Turing Test and Chatterbots :

The Turing Test is a test created by Alan Turing in 1950 which was originally designed to test the ability of a computer to think like a human. In the test, a person communicates with two entities, one of which is a human and one of which is a computer program. The person then has to determine which entity is the computer program. Chatterbots are computer programs designed to simulate conversation with humans. They are used in AI applications such as customer service and natural language processing. Chatterbots can be used to pass the Turing Test, as they are able to simulate human conversation.

The Turing Test is a test of a machine's ability to exhibit intelligent behavior equivalent to, or indistinguishable from, that of a human. It is a test for Artificial Intelligence (AI) and is also known as the "Imitation Game". The test was proposed by Alan Turing in 1950 and involved three participants: a computer, a human interrogator, and a human confederate. The interrogator was tasked with determining which of the other two participants was the computer.

In modern times, the Turing Test is often used to evaluate the intelligence of chatbots, or computer programs designed to simulate conversation with a human. These chatbots are programmed to understand natural language and respond in a way that is indistinguishable from a real human's response. If the chatbot is able to fool the interrogator into believing it is a human, then it is said to have passed the Turing Test.

The Turing Test is a test of artificial intelligence (AI). It was proposed by Alan Turing in 1950 and involves a human judge conversing with two entities, one of which is a human and the other an AI computer. The judge then attempts to determine which of the two participants is the human and which is the AI.

Chatterbots are computer programs that simulate conversation with humans in natural language. They are often used for customer service, entertainment, and educational applications. Chatterbots can be used in the Turing Test to simulate a human conversation, allowing the judge to determine the AI's ability to pass the test.

The Turing Test is a method of determining whether or not a computer is capable of demonstrating intelligent behavior. It was proposed by Alan Turing in 1950 and tests a machine's ability to exhibit intelligent behavior equivalent to, or indistinguishable from, a human. In the Turing Test, a human judge engages in a natural language conversation with two participants, one a computer and the other a human. If the judge cannot reliably tell the difference between the computer and the human, then the computer is said to have passed the test.

Chatterbots are a type of AI software that is designed to simulate natural conversations with a human. They are programmed to respond to specific inputs, using natural language processing techniques to understand and respond to the input. The most popular chatterbots are designed to answer questions and take part in small talk conversations. Chatterbots can be used to provide customer service, offer help with tasks, and engage in basic conversations. They can also be used to conduct Turing tests.

Agents Terminology :

1. Agent: An autonomous program that can act on behalf of a user or other program to perform tasks, such as search and retrieval, or data mining.

2. Intelligent Agent: An agent that uses artificial intelligence techniques to increase its ability to complete tasks.

3. Learning Agent: An agent that is able to improve its performance over time by adapting to changing environments and user preferences.

4. Autonomous Agent: An agent that is capable of acting independently and making decisions without requiring external input or human intervention.

5. Multi-agent System: A system composed of multiple agents that interact and work together to achieve a common goal.

6. Swarm Intelligence: A type of artificial intelligence based on the collective behavior of large groups of agents.

7. Negotiation Agent: An agent that is capable of autonomously engaging in negotiations with other agents to reach mutually beneficial outcomes.

8. Utility Function: A mathematical function used to determine the value of a given action or set of actions for an agent.

Task Classification of AI :

The task classification of AI can be divided into three main categories:

1. Knowledge Representation and Reasoning: This type of task involves representing knowledge in a computer-friendly format and then using inference algorithms to reason about it. Examples include automated theorem

proving and planning.

2. Machine Learning: This type of task involves creating algorithms that can learn from data. Examples include supervised learning, unsupervised learning, reinforcement learning, and deep learning.

3. Natural Language Processing: This type of task involves understanding and generating natural language. Examples include speech recognition, text understanding, and text generation.

CHAPTER TWO

Programming With AI

Artificial intelligence is a powerful tool that can be used to create automated solutions to complex problems. AI can be used to solve problems such as image recognition, natural language processing, speech recognition, and more. AI can also be used to create intelligent agents that can interact with users and carry out tasks autonomously. AI can be used to automate mundane tasks, enabling organizations to focus on higher-level goals and objectives.

Programming with AI is the process of using Artificial Intelligence (AI) to create computer programs that can analyze data, learn from it, and make decisions based on their findings. This can be done through a variety of methods, such as machine learning, deep learning, and natural language processing. AI-powered programs can be used for a number of tasks, such as predicting stock prices, recognizing patterns in images, and providing automated customer support.

AI programming is a branch of computer science that deals with creating intelligent computer programs. AI programming involves the use of algorithms and techniques such as machine learning, natural language processing, computer vision, and robotics to create programs that can act and make decisions like humans.

AI programming is used in many different fields, such as healthcare, finance, video games, and robotics. AI programming is essential for the development of autonomous systems, such as self-driving cars, that can make decisions and take action without the need for human intervention.

Programming with AI involves using AI algorithms and models to create programs that can process data and make decisions. This could involve creating autonomous robots, machine learning systems, or natural language processing applications. Using AI algorithms and models allows programmers to create more complex and intelligent programs that can learn and adapt to changing conditions.

The New Connectionism :

The new connectionism in AI is a branch of research which focuses on using artificial neural networks to study cognition and intelligence. These neural networks are inspired by the way the brain works, and by using them AI systems can learn about the environment and make decisions based on what they learn. This branch of AI is still relatively new, but it has already been used to develop technologies such as self-driving cars and facial recognition software. Its potential applications are vast, and it is one of the most exciting areas of research in AI today.

The New Connectionism is a field of research that seeks to build bridges between neuroscience and artificial intelligence (AI). It attempts to bring together the best of both worlds, combining the power of AI with the insights of neuroscience to create a more powerful, intelligent, and robust form of AI. This research seeks to create a better understanding of how the brain works and how AI can be better designed to mimic and augment its processes. It focuses on connections between the brain and AI, such as how neural networks can be adapted to better understand data and how AI can learn from the brain's processes. The goal of the research is to develop a better understanding of the relationship between the two, which could lead to the development of more effective and efficient AI.

The New Connectionism is an emerging field of cognitive science that seeks to better understand how the brain works by combining neuroscience, artificial intelligence, and machine learning. It focuses on the use of neural networks, which are computer models that mimic the workings of the brain. These models are used to study the structure and functions of the brain, such as its ability to learn, store memories, and process information. It has also been used to create applications such as robotics and computer vision. The New Connectionism is an exciting field of research that has the potential to revolutionize our understanding of the brain and its capabilities.

The New Connectionism in AI is a relatively new approach to Artificial Intelligence (AI) that is based on neural network models. This type of AI attempts to replicate the workings of the human brain by using connectionist models. These models are based on artificial neurons, which are nodes of computation that are interconnected in a network. This type of AI is motivated by the idea that the connections between neurons are the basis of learning and memory, and that the same principles could be used to create intelligent machines. This type of AI has been used to create powerful machine learning algorithms, such as Deep Learning, which have been applied to tasks such as image and voice recognition.

The New Connectionism in AI is an approach to artificial intelligence (AI) that focuses on building systems that are based on artificial neural networks. It is based on the idea of using a neural network to simulate the behavior of a biological brain, and has been used to create systems that can learn, reason, and make decisions. The New Connectionism has been used to develop autonomous robots, natural language processing systems, and self-adaptive intelligent systems. Additionally, it has been used to improve existing AI applications such as image processing, machine learning, and robotics. By connecting nodes in a network, artificial neural networks can learn from their environment and adapt to new situations. This approach allows AI systems to become increasingly adaptive and intelligent.

Reasoning Under Uncertainty :

Reasoning under uncertainty in AI involves using techniques such as probabilistic inference, Bayesian networks, Markov decision processes, and Monte Carlo simulations to develop AI systems that can reason and make decisions when faced with uncertain or incomplete information. This integration of uncertainty into AI systems is essential for creating intelligent machines that can successfully interact with the real world, where information is often uncertain or incomplete.

Probabilistic inference enables AI systems to make decisions that are based on incomplete information by assigning probabilities to possible outcomes. Bayesian networks allow AI systems to learn from data and make inferences based on probabilities; Markov decision processes allow AI systems to make decisions based on sequential information; and Monte Carlo simulations allow AI systems to explore a range of possible outcomes. By integrating these techniques, AI systems can make decisions or take actions in uncertain environments, thereby enabling them to be more effective in real-world applications.

Reasoning under uncertainty is the process of making decisions in the face of incomplete or uncertain information. It involves using logic, probability theory, and game theory to come to the best possible conclusion given the available evidence. It is an important part of decision-making in many fields, from business and economics to medicine and law. The goal is to identify the most likely outcome of a situation given the available data and to develop strategies to reduce the risk associated with the decision.

Reasoning under uncertainty is the process of making decisions and drawing conclusions about a given situation when there is doubt, lack of information, or incomplete data. It involves using a combination of logical reasoning, probability theory, and heuristics to make inferences and arrive at informed decisions. It is an important skill in many areas, including finance, economics, engineering, and medicine.

Reasoning under uncertainty in AI involves the use of algorithms and techniques to identify, represent, and reason about uncertain situations. It involves the use of probability theory and Bayesian networks to model and reason with uncertain data. It is an important part of AI research because it enables AI to make decisions that are robust to the presence of uncertainty and can be applied to a wide range of AI applications, such as robotics and natural language processing.

By using probability theory and Bayesian networks, AI can better represent and reason about situations where the data is uncertain or incomplete. For example, in a robotics application, AI can use this technique to identify objects in an image and make decisions about how to interact with them, despite uncertainty in the data.

Reasoning under uncertainty in AI is the process of making decisions and predictions in the face of incomplete or uncertain data. It is a core component of artificial intelligence and is used to improve the accuracy of predictions. This process requires AI systems to assess and identify the most appropriate decision given a set of available data, often making use of probabilities and logic to do so. The process is designed to enable AI systems to make decisions in a variety of contexts and to consider various sources of knowledge and evidence. The ability to reason under uncertainty helps AI systems to identify patterns and trends, to make inferences about unknown information, and to develop better strategies for problem-solving.

Distributed, Autonomous and Learning Agents :

Distributed agents in AI are autonomous agents that exist in a distributed environment, where multiple agents are able to interact and cooperate with each other in order to achieve a common goal. The agents are typically self-governing, meaning they can make decisions on their own and communicate with other agents.

Distributed agents are used in many AI systems, such as robotic control, multi-agent systems, distributed search algorithms, and distributed databases. Distributed agents can be used in applications that require collaboration and coordination between multiple agents, such as task scheduling, resource allocation, and distributed problem solving.

Distributed agents can be used to create autonomous and self-learning systems, as well as for agent-based simulations. They can be used to provide flexible, dynamic, and adaptive solutions to complex problems, and can be used to increase the scalability and robustness of AI systems.

Distributed agents in AI are agents that are designed to operate in an environment composed of multiple, distributed agents that interact with each other. They are designed to work in a decentralized environment and are capable of learning, problem-solving, and decision-making in a distributed environment. They are typically used in complex tasks such as multi-agent systems, robotic systems, or distributed computing. They are used to improve overall system performance, by allowing agents to share knowledge and reduce the complexity of individual tasks.

Autonomous agents in AI are computer programs or robots that are capable of sensing, planning, adapting, and acting in order to achieve specific goals. Autonomous agents are able to make decisions and carry out tasks independently of human intervention. Autonomous agents are used in a variety of applications, including robotics, search and rescue, logistics, and autonomous navigation. Autonomous agents can also be used in AI-based decision-making systems, where they are able to make decisions on behalf of people or organizations.

Autonomous agents are computer systems that act independently in an environment in order to achieve a specific goal. They are capable of making decisions, learning from their environment, and adapting to changes in order to achieve their goals. Autonomous agents are used in Artificial Intelligence (AI) to simulate human behavior and develop intelligent systems.

Autonomous agents are used in a variety of applications such as robotics, computer vision, natural language processing, and autonomous vehicles. Autonomous agents have the potential to reduce human labor in many tasks, as they can be programmed to take on more complex and difficult tasks. Autonomous agents can also be used to provide solutions to problems that may be difficult or impossible for humans to solve. Autonomous agents are used in many areas of AI, including machine learning, deep learning, and reinforcement learning.

Reinforcement Learning (RL) is a type of artificial intelligence that allows software agents and machines to automatically determine the ideal behavior within a specific context, in order to maximize its performance. RL is one of the three basic machine learning paradigms, alongside supervised learning and unsupervised learning.

Reinforcement learning algorithms allow an agent to learn in an environment by trial and error. In this type of learning, the agent is not told which action to take, but instead must discover which action yields the maximum reward. The agent must learn by executing different actions and receiving feedback from the environment. The reward signal indicates how well the agent is performing, and the agent must use this signal to update its knowledge and adjust its behavior.

Reinforcement learning algorithms can be used in a variety of contexts, including robotics, gaming, and financial trading. These algorithms are often used in the development of autonomous agents that are capable of making decisions in complex, dynamic environments.

Learning agents in Artificial Intelligence (AI) are computer programs that use algorithms to learn from their environment and improve their performance over time. These agents can be given a task and will, through trial and error, learn how to complete that task. For example, a learning agent in a game of chess can learn the rules of the game, develop strategies, and eventually become a strong player. Similarly, a learning agent in an AI system can learn to recognize patterns, make decisions, and interact with its environment in an intelligent manner.

Difference between Human and Machine Intelligence:

Human intelligence is the ability to think, learn, reason, make decisions and use experience to solve problems. It is largely based on the ability to understand complex concepts and make use of them in a practical way. Human intelligence is also based on the ability to recognize patterns and draw logical conclusions from them.

Human intelligence is the ability to learn, think, and reason. It involves the ability to comprehend complex ideas, develop ideas, think abstractly, and use knowledge to solve problems. Human intelligence also involves the ability to adapt and learn from experience, recognize and understand emotions, develop relationships, and make decisions.

Human intelligence, on the other hand, is the capacity for logical thought, understanding, self-awareness, learning, emotional knowledge, reasoning, planning, creativity, and problem-solving. It is based on the mental faculties of a human being and their ability to combine and apply knowledge. Human intelligence is based on the ability to use abstract concepts, understand complex relationships, and think logically. Humans are also able to use experience to draw meaningful conclusions and solve problems.

Human intelligence is the capacity to think and reason, understand concepts and ideas, draw conclusions, and use experience to solve problems. It is based on the unique ability of humans to use the abstract and creative parts of their brains to think and reason. Human intelligence has the capability to combine prior knowledge and experience, think creatively, and make decisions. It is also capable of understanding complex concepts and abstract ideas.

Machine intelligence, on the other hand, is the ability of a computer or robot to perform tasks that would normally require human intelligence. It is largely based on algorithms and programming code that enable the machine to make decisions and solve problems based on the data it collects. Machine intelligence typically relies on the ability to recognize patterns and draw logical conclusions from them, but it lacks the ability to understand complex concepts and use experience to solve problems.

Machine intelligence is the ability of a computer or machine to perform tasks traditionally associated with human intelligence. It includes the ability to use data to solve problems, recognize patterns and trends, understand language, and interact with its environment. Machines are programmed to respond to certain inputs and can learn from experience, but they lack the ability to think abstractly, form meaningful relationships, and make intuitive decisions.

Human intelligence is the ability to think, reason, and problem solve, while machine intelligence is the ability of a computer or other machine to perform tasks traditionally requiring human intelligence. Human intelligence is based on intuition, experience, and creative problem solving, while machine intelligence is based on algorithms and data-driven decisions. Human intelligence is contextual, meaning it can take into account multiple variables and parameters to come to a conclusion, while machine intelligence is more limited in its ability to make decisions and is limited by the data and algorithms it is given. Human intelligence is also able to adapt and learn from mistakes, while machine intelligence relies on programming and data to learn from mistakes.

Machine intelligence (or artificial intelligence) is the ability of machines to process and interpret information, learn from data, and make decisions or take actions independently. It is a broad field of study that focuses on the development of algorithms and systems that can think, reason, and act like humans. Machine intelligence can be used to automate processes, improve decision-making, and create new products and services. Examples of machine intelligence applications include facial recognition, self-driving cars, natural language processing, and robotics.

Machine intelligence is the ability of a machine to think and learn in a manner similar to that of a human. It involves the use of artificial intelligence (AI) algorithms to enable a computer, robot, or other machine to process information, reason, and make decisions in the same way as a human would. In addition, machine intelligence can also involve the use of deep learning algorithms, which are based on neural networks, to allow machines to recognize patterns and make decisions.

CHAPTER THREE

Research Areas of AI

The following are leading research areas of AI
1. Natural Language Processing (NLP)
2. Computer Vision
3. Machine Learning
4. Robotics
5. Artificial Neural Networks
6. Automated Planning and Scheduling
7. Knowledge Representation
8. Knowledge Engineering
9. Expert Systems
10. Automated Reasoning
11. Natural Language Generation
12. Cognitive Computing
13. Autonomous Agents
14. Decision Making & Optimization
15. Multi-Agent Systems
16. Speech Recognition
17. Generative Models
18. Reinforcement Learning

Natural Language Processing (NLP) :

Natural Language Processing (NLP) in AI is a field of study that focuses on the interaction between computers and human language. NLP allows computers to understand, interpret, and manipulate human language in order to gain meaningful insights from text. It is used in a variety of areas such as machine translation, automatic summarization, text classification, and question answering. NLP algorithms use techniques such as natural language processing, natural language understanding, and natural language generation to enable computers to interpret and reason about human language.

Natural language processing (NLP) is a subfield of computer science, artificial intelligence, and linguistics concerned with the interactions between computers and human (natural) languages. As such, NLP is related to the area of human-computer interaction. Many challenges in NLP involve natural language understanding, that is, the ability to do things such as determine the syntactic structure of sentences, determine the meaning of words in context, and determine the overall meaning of sentences. NLP also involves natural language generation, which is the ability to generate meaningful and grammatically correct sentences from a given set of input data. NLP is used in many applications, such as question answering, machine translation, information extraction, dialogue systems, and text summarization.

Natural Language Processing (NLP) is a field of Artificial Intelligence (AI) that focuses on the interactions between computers and humans using natural language. It is used to analyze, understand, and generate human language in a smart and useful way. NLP techniques are used for tasks such as automatic summarization, text classification, sentiment analysis, topic segmentation, and language translation.

Natural Language Processing (NLP) is a branch of Artificial

Intelligence (AI) that deals with the interaction between computers and human (natural) languages. It helps computers understand, interpret, and manipulate human language. It is used to analyze text, audio, and other natural language data. NLP enables computers to understand the meaning of human language and to respond in a meaningful way. It can be used for tasks such as machine translation, text classification, question answering, and document summarization.

Natural Language Processing (NLP) is a branch of Artificial Intelligence (AI) that deals with understanding and processing human language. NLP algorithms are used to analyze and interpret natural language, and can be used to automate processes such as text summarization, sentiment analysis, and text categorization. NLP can also be used to develop applications such as chatbots, virtual assistants, and machine translation.

Machine Learning :

Machine Learning can be used in many different ways. It can be used for predictive analytics, object recognition, natural language processing, image recognition, and even robotics. It can be used to automate tasks, such as driving a car, making decisions, or recognizing objects. It can also be used to create personalized user experiences, such as helping customers find the right product or offering personalized recommendations. Additionally, machine learning can be used to develop more accurate models for forecasting, such as predicting stock prices or weather patterns.

Machine learning is a type of artificial intelligence (AI) that provides computers with the ability to learn without being explicitly programmed. Machine learning focuses on the development of computer programs that can teach themselves to grow and change when exposed to new data. The process of machine learning is similar to that of data mining, as both involve searching through large amounts of data to look for patterns and making decisions based on those patterns. The primary difference between the two is that machine learning is concerned with the development of computer programs that can learn and adapt to new data, while data mining involves searching through large amounts of data to look for patterns.

The goal of machine learning is to create models that can learn from data and make predictions about future data. This is done by using algorithms that learn from data, such as neural networks and gradient boosting machines. These algorithms are used to create models that can identify patterns in data and detect anomalies. By using these models, businesses can better understand their data and make better decisions. Machine learning can also be used for tasks such as natural language processing and computer vision.

Machine learning is a subset of artificial intelligence (AI) that focuses on the development of algorithms and computer systems that are able to learn from data, identify patterns, and make decisions with minimal human intervention. It is used in a variety of applications, from predicting customer behavior to controlling autonomous vehicles. Machine learning algorithms are used to detect fraud, diagnose diseases, and predict traffic patterns.

Machine Learning is a subset of Artificial Intelligence (AI) that enables a system to learn from data sets and apply what it has learned to new data sets. It builds algorithms that can learn from and make predictions on data. Some common examples of Machine Learning include facial recognition, natural language processing, and handwriting recognition. By using Machine Learning, AI can make decisions and predictions based on data sets that it has been trained on.

Computer Vision :

Computer vision in AI refers to the ability of a computer to interpret and analyze images. It is a type of artificial intelligence (AI) that enables machines to identify objects, recognize patterns, and understand the physical environment around them. Computer vision technology is used in a variety of applications, such as autonomous vehicles, facial recognition, and medical imaging.

Computer vision is a field of study that enables computers to understand the contents of digital images and videos. It is a sub-field of artificial intelligence, where computers are programmed to gain a high-level understanding of digital images, videos, 3D models, and other data sources. This understanding is achieved through the use of algorithms to recognize patterns, detect objects, and track movement. Computer vision applications are used in a variety of fields, from medical imaging to autonomous vehicles.

Computer vision is a field of artificial intelligence and computer science that deals with how computers can be made to understand and interpret digital images and videos. It involves the development of algorithms and systems that can automatically process, analyze, and understand digital images, and then provide appropriate output. Computer vision is used in a wide range of applications, including facial recognition, object detection, motion estimation, and medical imaging.

Computer vision in AI is the use of computer algorithms to interpret, analyze, and understand digital images from the real world. Computer vision algorithms are used to detect objects, classify objects, and identify patterns in digital images. This technology is used in a wide range of applications, including facial recognition, object tracking, medical imaging, and autonomous vehicles.

Computer vision in AI is a field of study that focuses on creating software that can interpret and understand digital images. This technology can be used for a variety of applications including surveillance, image recognition, object detection, facial recognition, and robotics. Computer vision can be used to process data from cameras, images, and video and can help machines understand the world around them. AI can also be used to improve the accuracy of computer vision algorithms by learning from data.

Robotics :

Robotics in AI is the use of robots for artificial intelligence (AI) research and development. Robotics in AI involves the design, construction, and application of robots to solve various problems related to AI. This includes robotic agents that are able to interact with the environment, learn from their experience, and make decisions to achieve a goal. Robotics in AI also includes the development of new algorithms and approaches for teaching robots to act autonomously and efficiently. Robotics in AI can be used to develop robots for a wide range of applications, including medical diagnosis, object manipulation, navigation, and social interaction.

Robotics is the branch of engineering that deals with the design, construction, operation, and use of robots, as well as computer systems for their control, sensory feedback, and information processing. These technologies are used to develop machines that can substitute for humans and replicate human actions. Robotics is also used in STEM (science, technology, engineering, and mathematics) as a teaching aid.

Robotics is the engineering field that focuses on the design, construction, and operation of robots. Robotics deals with the development of machines that can substitute for humans and replicate human actions. Robotics technology is used to design and build robots that can be utilized in various applications, from manufacturing and assembly to medical and military uses. Robotics also involves the use of artificial intelligence (AI) to program robots to interact with their environment and complete tasks autonomously.

Robotics in AI is the use of robots to perform tasks that are typically done by humans. This includes tasks such as object recognition, navigation and manipulation, autonomous navigation, and other complex problem-solving tasks. AI can be used to power robots, allowing them to learn from experience and adapt to their environment. AI-powered robots can be used in a variety of applications, from industrial automation to healthcare and even space exploration. Additionally, AI can be used to develop more efficient and effective robots, which can be used in a variety of industries, from manufacturing to agriculture.

Robotics in AI is the application of artificial intelligence (AI) to robots. AI is used to create autonomous robots that can move and interact with their environment, as well as to make robots smarter, faster, and more efficient. AI is also used to develop robot arms, robot vision systems, robot navigation systems, and robot learning algorithms. Robotics in AI is an important field of study in the field of robotics, as it allows robots to interact more effectively with their environment and perform tasks more effectively.

AI technology is also being used to develop robots that can be used in medical and industrial applications.

Automation :

Automation in AI is the use of automated techniques to build intelligent systems. This includes techniques such as machine learning, natural language processing, and robotics. Automation in AI allows for more efficient and accurate processing of data, faster decision making and more accurate predictions. Automation also makes it easier to develop AI applications, as the automation can take care of mundane tasks that would otherwise require manual coding. In addition, automation can reduce the cost of development, as tasks that would require manual coding can be reduced or eliminated.

Automation is the use of technology to automate tasks, processes and operations that were previously carried out manually or with less advanced technology. Automation is used to increase efficiency, reduce costs, improve accuracy and enhance safety. Automation can help reduce the amount of human resources needed to complete a task and can increase the accuracy and speed of the process. Automation can also be used to help with decision making by providing data and analysis. Automation can help to reduce the risk of errors and increase consistency.

Automation is the use of technology, such as computers, robots, and artificial intelligence, to reduce or eliminate the need for manual labor in a variety of tasks. Automation can be used in a wide range of industries, from manufacturing to healthcare, to make processes more efficient and cost-effective. Automation can be utilized to improve customer service, increase accuracy, reduce costs, and improve safety in a variety of settings. Automation can also help to streamline complex processes and increase productivity.

Automation is becoming increasingly popular as businesses look for ways to save time and money while providing better service to their customers. Automation can help to increase efficiency, reduce errors, and reduce labor costs.

Automation in AI is a way of utilizing AI technology to automate processes and workflows that are traditionally done manually. By automating mundane tasks, AI can free up resources to focus on more complex tasks, while also reducing the risk of human error. Examples of AI automation include natural language processing, predictive analytics, computer vision, and robotics.

Automation in AI refers to the use of software programs and algorithms to automate certain tasks that would normally require manual effort from a human. This automation can be used to increase efficiency, reduce costs, and improve accuracy. Automation can be applied to tasks such as natural language processing, image recognition, pattern recognition, and more. Automation can also be used to automate mundane tasks such as data entry and data analysis. Automation in AI can help to speed up the process of building and training AI models, reducing the amount of time needed to complete a project.

Expert Systems :

Expert systems are a type of Artificial Intelligence (AI) technology that utilizes knowledge from experts in a particular field in order to mimic human reasoning and process data. They are programs that use a combination of machine learning, natural language processing, and rules-based logic to solve complex problems. The goal of an expert system is to create a system that can provide decision support and expert advice to users. Expert systems are used in a variety of applications such as medical diagnosis, financial analysis, engineering design, and customer service.

Expert systems are computer-based systems that offer advice and solutions to complex problems, usually within a specific domain. They are designed to emulate the decision-making process of a human expert, and they typically include a knowledge base of facts and heuristics, a reasoning engine, and a user interface. Expert systems are used in various fields, such as medicine, engineering, finance, and law.

Expert systems are computer systems that emulate the decision-making abilities of a human expert. They use a combination of artificial intelligence (AI) and knowledge engineering to provide solutions to complex problems. They are designed to provide solutions to problems that are difficult for a human to solve or require a great deal of expertise. Expert systems are used in a variety of fields, including medicine, finance, engineering, and law. They are used to diagnose and treat medical conditions, identify financial risks, design engineering systems, and interpret legal documents.

Expert systems are computer programs designed to emulate the decision-making abilities of a human expert. They are typically used to solve complex problems which are beyond the capability of traditional programming techniques. Expert systems use a combination of artificial intelligence techniques such as search algorithms, natural language processing, and knowledge representation to generate solutions. Expert systems can be used in a variety of applications, from medicine and engineering to finance and marketing.

Expert systems are computer programs which attempt to emulate the decision-making ability of a human expert. They are designed to solve complex problems by reasoning through bodies of knowledge, using a combination of facts, heuristics, and inference. Expert systems have been used in many fields of AI, from natural language processing to robotics. They are especially well suited for tasks that require a high degree of accuracy and consistency, such as medical diagnosis and financial analysis.

Neural Networks :

Neural networks are a type of artificial intelligence that is based on the structure of the human brain and the way it processes information. Neural networks are made up of artificial neurons, or nodes, which are connected to each other in layers. Each node is responsible for processing a certain type of input and then outputting the result. They are able to learn from their environment and adjust their internal structure to better process the data they receive. Neural networks are used for a variety of tasks, such as image recognition, natural language processing, and machine translation.

Neural networks are a set of algorithms, modeled loosely after the human brain, that are designed to recognize patterns. They interpret sensory data through a kind of machine perception, labeling or clustering raw input. The patterns they recognize are numerical, contained in vectors, into which all real-world data, be it images, sound, text or time series, must be translated. Neural networks help us cluster and classify. They can be used to find relationships and correlations between inputs and outputs. They can even be used to generate music or paint.

Neural networks are a class of machine learning algorithms modeled after the human brain. They are composed of multiple layers of interconnected nodes which activate nonlinear functions as they process input data. Neural networks can be used for a variety of tasks such as classification, regression, and clustering. They are typically used for supervised learning tasks, where the input data is labeled and the desired output is known. The goal of the neural network is to learn a set of weights and biases which map the input data to the desired output.

Neural networks are a type of artificial intelligence that uses interconnected layers of artificial neurons to process information. Neural networks are inspired by the biological neural networks that make up the human brain, and they have been used to solve a wide variety of problems in various fields, from computer vision to natural language processing. Neural networks are commonly used for supervised learning tasks such as classification, regression, and clustering, as well as for unsupervised learning tasks such as feature extraction and dimensionality reduction.

Neural networks are a type of artificial intelligence algorithm modeled after the way the human brain works. They are used to recognize patterns and classify data, and can be used for a variety of tasks such as image recognition, natural language processing, and decision-making. Neural networks can learn from experience and adapt to changing environments, making them very powerful in a wide range of applications.

Fuzzy Logic :

Fuzzy logic is a form of AI that uses a mathematical system of fuzzy set theory to approximate and simulate human reasoning. It is based on the idea that things are not always black and white, but instead can have varying degrees of membership in a set. Fuzzy logic systems are used to make decisions, solve problems, and analyze data sets. In AI, fuzzy logic is used to make decisions based on uncertain or imprecise data, such as facial recognition, self-driving cars, and natural language processing.

Fuzzy logic is a form of artificial intelligence that attempts to mimic the way humans think and make decisions. It is based on the idea that instead of making decisions based on clear-cut rules, fuzzy logic allows for more freedom in decision-making. This freedom is achieved through the use of fuzzy sets, which are sets of data with varying degrees of membership. Fuzzy logic is used in a variety of applications including robotics, control systems, and natural language processing.

Fuzzy logic is a form of many-valued logic in which the truth values of variables may be any real number between 0 and 1. It is employed to handle the concept of partial truth, where the truth value may range between completely true and completely false. By contrast, in Boolean logic, the truth values of variables may only be the integer values 0 or 1. Fuzzy logic has been extended to handle the concept of linguistic variables, defined as variables whose values are words or phrases in a natural language, like low, medium, or high. It has also been applied to complex problems in many fields, including artificial intelligence, control theory, decision theory, expert systems, information retrieval, law, linguistics, philosophy, robotics, and video games.

Fuzzy logic is a form of many-valued logic in which the truth values of variables may be any real number between 0 and 1. It is employed to handle the concept of partial truth, where the truth value may range between completely true and completely false. By contrast, in Boolean logic, the truth values of variables may only be the integer values 0 or 1. Fuzzy logic has been extended to handle the concept of linguistic variables, defined as variables whose values are words or sentences in a natural or artificial language. Fuzzy logic has been applied to many fields, from control theory to artificial intelligence.

Fuzzy logic is a form of artificial intelligence that uses fuzzy set theory to approximate a given problem in order to arrive at a solution. It is based on the idea that there is no clear boundary between true and false, but rather a continuum of possibilities in between. Fuzzy logic allows the computer to make decisions based on imprecise data, such as human language, sensory inputs, and other ambiguous information. This makes it a powerful tool for solving complex problems that would otherwise require an exhaustive search of all possible solutions.

Fuzzy logic is a form of artificial intelligence (AI) that deals with the concept of partial truth, where variables can have values between 0 and 1, representing degrees of truth. It is used to interpret complex data sets and to make decisions based on multiple inputs. Fuzzy logic can be used in a wide range of applications, such as data mining, natural language processing, robotics, and financial decision-making. Fuzzy logic can be used to create intelligent systems that can provide more accurate and reliable results than traditional methods.

Speech Recognition :

Speech recognition is a technology that allows machines to recognize and respond to human speech. It is used in various applications such as virtual assistants, automated customer service agents, voice-controlled home automation systems, and more. Speech recognition technology can understand spoken words and convert them into text that can be used to perform tasks such as answering questions, providing directions, making recommendations, and more.

Speech recognition is the process of automatically recognizing spoken words and converting them into a written or machine-readable form. It is a type of artificial intelligence that allows computers to recognize and respond to human speech. Speech recognition systems are used in many applications, including voice user interfaces, automatic speech recognition (ASR) systems, voice search, voice-enabled applications, and more.

Speech recognition is a technology that enables a machine or computer to identify words and phrases in spoken language and convert them into a machine-readable format. It is also known as automatic speech recognition (ASR), computer speech recognition or speech-to-text (STT). It is widely used in various applications such as voice-controlled user interfaces, voice search, voice commands, voice biometrics and natural language processing.

Speech recognition in AI is the process of using computer algorithms and software to recognize spoken words and turn them into a digital format. AI-based speech recognition technology is used in a variety of applications, from virtual assistants and customer service bots to automated transcription services and smart home appliances. The technology is constantly improving, resulting in higher accuracy and faster response times.

Speech recognition is a technology that enables computers to recognize spoken words and convert them into written or digital text. It is a form of artificial intelligence (AI) that has been around since the early 1950s, although it has become increasingly sophisticated in recent years. Speech recognition can be used to transcribe spoken conversations into text, to enable hands-free computer operation, and to enable voice-based search and control of computers.

Evolutionary Computing :

Evolutionary computing is a branch of artificial intelligence that uses evolutionary algorithms to solve complex problems. It mimics natural evolution in order to find solutions to difficult problems that may be too complex for traditional algorithms. It is used to optimize problem solutions by using a population of solutions that are modified through recombination and mutation, and then are selected based on their fitness (their ability to solve the problem).

Evolutionary computing is a type of artificial intelligence which is based on principles of evolutionary biology, such as mutation, recombination, and selection. It is used to solve complex problems by simulating the process of natural selection. It works by generating a series of solutions and selecting the best ones through a process of trial and error. The best solutions are then combined to create even better solutions, until a satisfactory result is found. Evolutionary computing is used in a variety of fields, including machine learning, robotics, and economics.

Evolutionary computing in AI is a form of artificial intelligence that uses evolutionary algorithms to generate and optimize solutions to complex problems. Evolutionary computing is based on the principles of evolutionary biology, where the best solutions are selected and bred to create the next generation of solutions. Evolutionary computing techniques can be used in a variety of AI applications, such as machine learning, robotics, data mining, natural language processing, and pattern recognition. These algorithms can be used to optimize parameters and design structures in order to find the best possible solution.

Evolutionary computing in AI is a branch of artificial intelligence that utilizes evolutionary algorithms to solve complex problems. It uses natural selection, mutation, recombination, and other evolutionary techniques to optimize a solution. Evolutionary computing has been used to solve problems in many areas, including robotics, machine learning, optimization, and game theory.

Evolutionary computing in AI is a type of artificial intelligence that uses evolutionary algorithms to find solutions to complex problems. Evolutionary computing works by simulating the process of evolution in order to find solutions to complex problems. Through this process, AI agents are able to identify patterns and trends that can be used to improve AI performance. Evolutionary computing also allows for more flexible and adaptive AI systems, as the evolutionary algorithms can be used to adjust the AI system as needed. This type of artificial intelligence is being used in a variety of fields such as robotics, finance, and game playing.

AI and Transportation :

Artificial intelligence (AI) and transportation have an important relationship. AI can be used to make transportation safer, more efficient, and more accessible. AI can be used to improve navigation, reduce traffic congestion, and automate vehicle operation. AI can also be used to monitor and analyze data from transportation systems, providing insights that can help improve safety, efficiency, and accessibility. AI can even be used to predict and prevent accidents. In the future, AI could be used to create autonomous vehicles, allowing people to travel without the need for a driver.

The use of AI in the transportation industry is becoming increasingly widespread. AI can be used to improve safety, efficiency, and convenience in a variety of ways. For example, AI-powered autonomous vehicles are being developed and tested for use on public roads. AI can also be used to improve traffic flow, route planning, and navigation systems. In addition, AI-powered predictive analytics can be used to anticipate and plan for changing traffic patterns. Finally, AI can be used to optimize the operations of public transportation systems, such as buses and subways.

AI is becoming increasingly integrated into the transportation sector as a way to create safer, more efficient, and more sustainable forms of transport. AI technologies are being used to improve the accuracy, safety, and efficiency of traffic monitoring and control, autonomous vehicles, and ride-sharing services. AI is also being used to develop predictive models to help manage traffic congestion, minimize emissions, and optimize the use of public transport. Additionally, AI systems are being used to detect and diagnose potential maintenance issues with vehicles, as well as to predict and anticipate customer needs. Ultimately, the use of AI in transportation is helping to create a more efficient, safe, and sustainable industry.

Machine Learning and Data Mining :

Machine Learning and Data Mining are related but distinct disciplines. Machine Learning is the study of algorithms that are able to learn from data, and it focuses on developing algorithms that can make predictions or classify data. Data Mining is the process of discovering patterns in large datasets and it focuses on discovering meaningful patterns in data. While the two disciplines are related, the focus and goals of each are distinct.

Machine Learning and Data Mining are two fields of Artificial Intelligence (AI) that have become popular in recent years. Machine learning is the ability of a computer system to learn from experience and data without being explicitly programmed. Data mining is the process of discovering patterns in large datasets by using sophisticated algorithms and statistical models.

The primary difference between machine learning and data mining is that machine learning focuses on using algorithms to make predictions and decisions, while data mining focuses on uncovering patterns and insights from data. While both are used to gain insights from data, machine learning is more focused on making predictions from data, while data mining is focused on discovering useful patterns from data.

In addition, data mining is often used to support machine learning algorithms. For example, a machine learning algorithm may use data mining to pre-process the data and extract features from the data set before making predictions. These features are then used by the machine learning algorithm to make its predictions.

In summary, machine learning and data mining are two fields of Artificial Intelligence (AI) that have become popular in recent years. While they have similar goals of gaining insights from data, they are different in that machine learning is focused on making predictions from data, while data mining is focused on discovering patterns and insights from data.

AI tools and vendors :

1. Amazon Machine Learning: Amazon Machine Learning (Amazon ML) is a service that enables developers to quickly and easily build predictive models and use them to generate predictions from their applications.

2. BigML: BigML is a cloud-based machine learning platform that enables data scientists and developers to build, deploy, and manage predictive models.

3. IBM Watson: IBM Watson is a powerful AI platform that helps organizations discover insights and build

solutions using natural language processing, machine learning, and deep learning.

4. H2O.ai: H2O.ai is an open source machine learning platform that enables enterprises to quickly develop and deploy models for predictive analytics.

5. Microsoft Azure ML: Microsoft Azure ML is a cloud-based platform for building, deploying, and managing predictive models.

6. Google Cloud ML Engine: Google Cloud ML Engine is a managed service that allows developers to build and deploy machine learning models to the cloud.

7. DataRobot: DataRobot is an automated machine learning platform that enables data scientists and developers to quickly and accurately build predictive models.

Genetic programming :

Genetic programming is a branch of artificial intelligence that uses the principles of natural selection and evolution to create programs. It is a search-based technique that starts with a set of random computer programs and uses an evolutionary algorithm to iteratively improve them. The goal is to find programs that solve a given problem. The evolutionary algorithm works by selecting the best programs, combining them to create new programs, and then testing the new programs to see if they are better than the original ones. The process is repeated until a program is found that solves the problem.

Genetic programming is a form of artificial intelligence which uses natural selection and genetic algorithms to generate computer programs which can solve problems. It is based on the principles of evolution and natural selection and works by creating an initial population of programs, then selecting the fittest programs to create a new generation which is then tested and the process is repeated until a solution is found. The programs are created using a set of instructions which define how the program should be constructed, and the population is modified by combining, mutating, and reproducing the programs.

Genetic programming (GP) is a type of evolutionary algorithm that uses genetic operators such as crossover and mutation to evolve a population of computer programs. GP starts with a randomly generated population of computer programs and uses a fitness function to evaluate how well each program performs a task. The fittest programs are selected to reproduce and create the next generation of programs. Over successive generations, the population of programs evolves to become better and better at performing the desired task. GP is used for a variety of applications, such as optimizing a trading strategy, finding new solutions to complex problems, and creating artificial intelligence applications.

Genetic programming is a type of artificial intelligence that uses evolutionary algorithms to generate computer programs that can solve complex problems. It works by creating a population of randomly generated computer programs, then using a combination of selection, crossover, and mutation to create new "offspring" programs that are more likely to solve the problem. The process is repeated until a program is generated that can solve the problem. Genetic programming is primarily used for optimization problems, but has been applied to a wide variety of tasks, including data mining and feature selection.

DATA MINING AND KNOWLEDGE DISCOVERY :

Data mining and knowledge discovery are two related but distinct processes used in the analysis of large sets of data. Data mining is the process of uncovering patterns and trends in large datasets by applying techniques such as classification, clustering, and regression. Knowledge discovery, on the other hand, is the process of extracting knowledge from large datasets using techniques such as machine learning and artificial intelligence. Data mining is often used to identify correlations among data sets, while knowledge discovery is used to uncover hidden patterns and relationships. Together, these two processes can be used to create powerful insights and inform decision-making.

Data mining and knowledge discovery are two closely related topics in the field of data science. Data mining is the process of discovering patterns in large datasets, while knowledge discovery is the process of extracting meaningful information from the data. Data mining involves the use of algorithms and statistical techniques to analyze the data to uncover hidden patterns and trends. These patterns and trends can then be used to make predictions and decisions. Knowledge discovery uses the same techniques but focuses on extracting knowledge from the data, such as relationships between variables and relationships between data points. Both data mining and knowledge discovery are important components of data science and can be used together to gain insights from data.

HYBRID INTELLIGENT SYSTEMS :

Hybrid intelligent systems are systems that combine artificial intelligence (AI) with other technologies to create a more accurate, adaptive, and intelligent solution. These systems are designed to solve complex problems and make decisions by combining the strengths of multiple AI technologies, such as neural networks, fuzzy logic, and evolutionary algorithms. Hybrid intelligent systems are used in a variety of applications, such as robotics, autonomous vehicles, and healthcare. They can also be used to improve customer service, optimize financial operations, and detect fraud.

Hybrid intelligent systems are a combination of two or more existing forms of artificial intelligence (AI) algorithms and techniques. These systems are used to solve complex problems that require the combination of multiple AI methods to achieve the desired results. Examples of hybrid intelligent systems include expert systems, fuzzy logic systems, neural networks, evolutionary algorithms, machine learning, and deep learning.

Hybrid intelligent systems are used to solve complex problems that require a combination of multiple AI algorithms and techniques. They are used in a variety of applications such as robotics, computer vision, natural language processing, and decision making. Hybrid intelligent systems are becoming increasingly popular due to their ability to integrate multiple AI approaches and provide better performance than individual AI methods.

Hybrid intelligent systems are computer systems that combine two or more distinct types of artificial intelligence systems to solve complex tasks. Examples of hybrid intelligent systems include expert systems, fuzzy logic systems and neural networks. Hybrid intelligent systems can be used to address complex tasks that cannot be solved using a single AI technique. This type of system is often used in applications such as robotics, machine vision, medical diagnosis, natural language processing, and financial forecasting.

ADAPTIVE NEURO-FUZZY INFERENCE SYSTEM :

The Adaptive Neuro-Fuzzy Inference System (ANFIS) is a type of artificial intelligence system that combines the principles of fuzzy logic and artificial neural networks. It is used for supervised learning in which a given set of input and output data is used to train the system. The system then uses the training data to make predictions or decisions based on new input data. ANFIS is used in a variety of applications, including medical diagnosis, robotics, and control systems. ANFIS can also be used to make predictions from chaotic or non-linear data.

Adaptive neuro-fuzzy inference systems (ANFIS) are a type of artificial neural network used to approximate arbitrary nonlinear functions. The goal of ANFIS is to combine the advantages of neural networks and fuzzy systems in order to create an approach that can adapt itself to a particular problem. ANFIS are used in many areas of artificial intelligence, such as machine learning, pattern recognition, and control systems. They are also used in areas such as robotics and computer vision. ANFIS are able to learn from data and can be used to create models of complex systems.

Adaptive Neuro-Fuzzy Inference System (ANFIS) is a type of artificial neural network which uses fuzzy logic principles to make predictions. It is a combination of both neural networks and fuzzy logic systems, and its aim is to approximate non-linear functions. ANFIS can be used to model complex problems that cannot be solved using traditional methods. It can also be used to classify data, identify patterns, and make decisions. ANFIS is well-suited for applications in control systems, data analysis, forecasting, and decision making.

Adaptive Neuro-Fuzzy Inference System (ANFIS) is a type of artificial neural network that combines fuzzy logic with a radial basis function network. ANFIS is a self-learning algorithm that is used for data modeling, classification, and prediction. It uses fuzzy logic to learn from the data and make predictions. ANFIS can be used for a wide range of applications such as medical diagnosis, stock market prediction, and weather forecasting. The main advantage of ANFIS over other machine learning algorithms is its ability to adapt and learn from data without requiring a priori knowledge. ANFIS also has a high level of accuracy and robustness, making it a powerful tool for data analysis.

NEURO-FUZZY SYSTEMS :

Neuro-fuzzy systems are a type of artificial intelligence system that combines the principles of fuzzy logic and neural networks. They are designed to mimic the way the human brain processes information, combining the ability to learn and adapt to new situations of neural networks with the ability to use rules and context to make decisions of fuzzy logic. Neuro-fuzzy systems have been used in a variety of applications including medical diagnosis, stock market prediction, image recognition, and natural language processing.

Neuro-fuzzy systems are a type of artificial intelligence technology that combines the principles of fuzzy logic and neural networks. They are used for modeling complex problems that are difficult to solve using traditional methods. These systems are built using algorithms that allow them to learn from data and make decisions based on that data. They are capable of handling uncertainty, ambiguity, and imprecise data with ease.

Neuro-fuzzy systems are used for a variety of applications, including medical diagnosis, financial forecasting, and control systems. They can also be used to identify patterns and anomalies in large datasets. Neuro-fuzzy systems are an important tool in the field of artificial intelligence and have been used to great success in many different industries.

Neuro-fuzzy systems are a combination of artificial neural networks and fuzzy logic. They are used to automate complex decision-making and data analysis tasks. They are used in many fields, such as control systems, decision support systems, data mining and data analysis, and robotics. Neuro-fuzzy systems are able to learn from examples and data, and develop a knowledge base of fuzzy rules. This allows them to make decisions and predictions based on the data.

Genetic programming :

Genetic programming is a form of artificial intelligence that uses evolutionary algorithms to generate computer programs that can solve a given problem. It starts with a set of randomly generated programs, which are then evaluated and modified based on their performance. The process is repeated until a program with the desired characteristics is found. Genetic programming can be used to solve a variety of problems, from predicting stock prices to identifying objects in images.

Genetic programming (GP) is a technique used in artificial intelligence that uses techniques inspired by evolutionary biology to generate computer programs that can solve a given problem. GP mimics biological evolution by randomly selecting, combining, and mutating computer programs until a suitable solution is found. The process begins by randomly generating a set of computer programs, called a population, which are then evaluated against a given problem.

The programs that perform best are kept, while the rest are discarded. The remaining programs are then randomly combined and mutated to create a new population, which is evaluated against the problem and the process repeated until a suitable solution is found. GP has been used to solve a wide range of problems ranging from robotics to engineering design.

Genetic programming is an evolutionary approach to solving problems. It is based on the concepts of biological evolution such as mutation, crossover, selection, and survival of the fittest. The idea is to use a population of computer programs that evolve over time through genetic operations. The programs are encoded in a form of representation such as a tree or graph, and each program is evaluated using a fitness function. The programs with the highest fitness are selected for reproduction, and the genetic operations are used to generate new programs. The process is repeated until a program is found that is able to solve the given problem.

Main advantages of genetic programming :

1. Automates the process of designing complex models: Genetic Programming (GP) automates the process of designing complex models by allowing programs to evolve and optimize themselves based on their performance. This eliminates the need for manual tuning and reduces the amount of time and effort required to build a model.

2. Handles large datasets: GP is able to handle large datasets and is capable of learning from them. It can learn from large amounts of data by combining different components to form a single, more effective program.

3. Handles non-linear problems: GP is well-suited for non-linear problems, as it can identify relationships between different variables and can form complex models without manual intervention.

4. Improves generalization: GP is able to improve generalization by creating models that are robust and can predict the behavior of unseen data.

5. Reduces manual tuning: GP eliminates the need for manual tuning, which is often time consuming and can introduce errors.

6. Automated hyperparameter tuning: Genetic programming can automatically tune the hyperparameters of a machine learning model, reducing the effort required to optimize a model.

Is mutation used in genetic programming?

Yes, mutation is a key component of genetic programming, which is a type of artificial intelligence that uses evolutionary algorithms to generate computer programs. In genetic programming, mutation is used to introduce random changes to the genetic code of a program in order to explore the search space and create new, potentially better solutions.

Virtual & Augmented Reality :

Virtual and Augmented Reality are two different technologies that are used to enhance the experience of viewing and interacting with the world. Virtual Reality (VR) is a computer-generated three-dimensional environment that can be interacted with and experienced in real time. This computer-generated environment is viewed through a headset and often requires the user to be completely immersed in the experience. Augmented Reality (AR) takes the real world and overlays it with computer-generated elements such as graphics, sound, and even touch. AR allows users to interact with the environment in a way that is not possible in the real world. Both technologies are being developed to create more immersive and realistic experiences that can be used in entertainment, gaming, education, and more.

Virtual Reality (VR) and Augmented Reality (AR) are technologies that allow users to interact with a computer-generated environment or physical environment respectively. VR immerses a user in a computer-generated environment, while AR adds virtual components to the physical environment. Both technologies can be used to create realistic and immersive experiences. These experiences can be used in a variety of applications, including gaming, education, entertainment, and training.

Virtual reality (VR) and augmented reality (AR) are two different forms of technology. Virtual reality immerses users in a completely simulated environment, while augmented reality layers digital elements onto the real world. Virtual reality systems use headsets that provide a 360-degree view of a virtual environment. Augmented reality systems use devices such as smartphones or smart glasses to overlay digital content onto the real world. VR and AR have a wide range of applications in gaming, education, medicine, and more.

Metaverse Technology :

Metaverse technology is a type of virtual reality system that enables users to interact with and explore a simulated environment. This type of technology includes the use of 3D graphics, artificial intelligence, and advanced networking techniques. Metaverse technology can be used to create virtual worlds, where users can interact with each other and with virtual objects. It is also used to create virtual environments for gaming and educational purposes. Metaverse technology is also being used to facilitate business transactions, such as making online purchases and trading stocks.

Metaverse Technology is a form of virtual reality technology that has the potential to provide users with an immersive, three-dimensional experience. Metaverse technology is based on the idea of creating a virtual world that is populated with objects, characters, and environments that can be interacted with in real-time by multiple users. Metaverse technology is currently being used in gaming, educational applications, and business applications such as virtual meetings, conferences, and training sessions. The long-term potential of Metaverse technology is to create a virtual world that can be used to replicate real-world scenarios, allowing virtual meetings, conferences, and training sessions to be held in a virtual space that is indistinguishable from the physical world.

Metaverse technology is a type of virtual world technology that allows users to interact in an online, 3D environment. It is based on the concept of a "metaverse," which is a virtual world made up of different interconnected virtual environments. This type of technology allows users to create their own virtual identities, communicate with others, and explore the many worlds available. The technology also allows users to build their own virtual items, create and customize their own virtual environment, and even purchase virtual goods and services. Metaverse technology is commonly used in video games, virtual reality experiences, and social networks.

Internet of Things :

The Internet of Things (IoT) is a term used to describe the

network of physical objects (devices, vehicles, buildings and other items) that are embedded with software, sensors, and other technologies to enable them to connect and exchange data with each other. This data can then be shared with other systems and used to control, monitor and automate tasks. Examples of IoT include smart home systems, connected cars and automated factory equipment.

The Internet of Things (IoT) is a term used to describe a network of connected physical objects that are able to collect and exchange data. These objects, or "things", can range from a range of everyday objects, such as lightbulbs, to more complex systems, such as autonomous vehicles. The IoT is made possible due to the proliferation of sensors, actuators, and other smart devices that can be connected to the Internet, as well as the development of powerful analytics and artificial intelligence (AI) technologies. By connecting these devices and systems, the IoT is creating a world where objects can be monitored, controlled, and automated in a way that was previously impossible. The IoT is transforming the way in which businesses operate, and is opening up new possibilities for industries such as healthcare, manufacturing, and energy.

The Internet of Things (IoT) is a network of physical objects or "things" embedded with electronics, software, sensors, and connectivity to enable it to collect and exchange data. It connects physical objects to the internet to enable them to send and receive data, making them "smart" and interactive. Examples of IoT include smart home appliances, connected cars, and wearables such as smart watches.

Deep Learning in Healthcare :

Deep learning is an area of artificial intelligence (AI) that focuses on creating algorithms that can teach themselves and improve accuracy with data over time. It can be used to analyze and interpret large datasets, and is increasingly being applied in the field of healthcare. Deep learning can be used to improve diagnosis accuracy, reduce healthcare costs, and provide personalized treatments. It can also be used to create more efficient algorithms for managing medical records, improve patient care, and enable faster drug discovery. Additionally, deep learning can help to detect and diagnose diseases, predict outcomes, and recommend treatments.

Deep learning is a type of machine learning algorithm that mimics the structure and function of the brain's neural networks. It is being applied in a wide range of industries from finance to healthcare. In healthcare, deep learning is being used to provide doctors with more accurate diagnostics, to improve the accuracy of medical image analysis, and to develop personalized treatments for patients. Deep learning can also be applied to medical data such as the electronic health records (EHRs) of patients, enabling doctors to gain insights into a patient's health history and predict their future health. Deep learning can also be used to automate administrative tasks such as billing and coding, allowing doctors to spend more time with patients. Ultimately, the goal of deep learning in healthcare is to improve patient outcomes by providing more accurate diagnoses, safer treatments, and better care.

Deep Learning in Healthcare is a relatively new field that has the potential to revolutionize diagnosis, treatments, and healthcare overall. Deep learning is the process of using large datasets and algorithms to build predictive models. It is a subset of AI that can automatically detect patterns and learn from data, allowing it to make decisions or predictions with minimal or no human involvement. Deep learning has been used in healthcare to improve patient diagnosis, treatment, and outcomes, as well as to reduce healthcare costs and improve overall efficiency.

For example, deep learning can be used to detect diseases, diagnose illnesses, predict patient outcomes, and personalize treatments. It can also be used to develop drug delivery technologies, streamline clinical trials, and identify potential drug targets. Additionally, deep learning can be used to analyze data from medical imaging, text documents, and other sources to find correlations between different diseases and treatments. With its increasing use in healthcare, deep learning has the potential to significantly improve patient outcomes, reduce costs, and improve overall healthcare.

Big Data :

Big Data is a term used to describe the large collection of data that is too complex to process with traditional data processing applications. It is used to identify patterns and trends in large datasets. It is used to create business intelligence and to provide insights into customer behavior and market trends. Big Data is used in a variety of industries, including healthcare, finance, retail, and government.

Big Data is a term used to describe the large and complex amount of data that organisations are now able to collect. This data can come from a variety of sources, such as social media, websites, sensors, and more. With the advent of new technologies, organisations have access to large volumes of data, and the challenge is to make sense of it and use it to inform decisions. Companies are increasingly using Big Data to improve their operations and gain competitive advantages. Big Data analytics enable organisations to identify trends, forecast outcomes, and gain insights into customer behaviour. As Big Data becomes more accessible and cost-effective, it is becoming an essential tool for businesses looking to stay ahead of the competition.

Big data is a term used to describe large, complex data sets that are difficult to manage and process using traditional data processing applications. Big data can come from many sources, including social media, web logs, sensors, and transactional applications. Big data is typically analyzed to uncover patterns and trends, leading to new insights and understanding. Companies are increasingly using big data technology to make better decisions, increase efficiency, and gain competitive advantages.

Hyper Automation :

Hyper automation is an approach to automation that uses a combination of tools, including artificial intelligence (AI), robotic process automation (RPA), and machine learning (ML). It is used to automate tasks that are either too complex or too time-consuming for human employees to handle. Hyper automation is used to streamline and optimize processes, reduce costs, and improve the customer experience.

Hyper Automation is an emerging technology that combines artificial intelligence, machine learning, and robotic process automation to automate complex business processes. It allows businesses to automate the end-to-end process, from capturing data to analyzing it and making decisions. Hyper Automation helps businesses in reducing operational costs, increasing efficiency, and improving customer service. It is also used to streamline decision-making processes, identify patterns, and gain insights into customer behavior.

Hyper automation is a process used to automate and integrate multiple technology components to complete a complex task. It involves the use of artificial intelligence (AI) and robotic process automation (RPA) to automate manual processes, identify improvements, and create more efficient workflows. Hyper automation helps organizations to reduce costs, improve accuracy, and increase productivity. This can be done by automating mundane tasks and eliminating manual errors. Additionally, hyper automation enables businesses to leverage data from multiple sources to gain insights and make more informed decisions.

Blockchain Technology :

Blockchain technology is a type of digital ledger that records and stores data in a secure, distributed, and decentralized manner. It works like a chain of digital blocks, where each block is linked to the next one, and contains a cryptographic hash of the previous one. The data stored in blockchain is immutable, meaning it cannot be changed or deleted without the permission of all the parties involved. Blockchain technology is used for a variety of applications, ranging from cryptocurrency to smart contracts, and more.

Blockchain technology is a decentralized, distributed, and immutable digital ledger of economic transactions. It is powered by a distributed network of computers that use cryptography to secure and verify each transaction, making it virtually impossible to tamper with. This technology has the potential to revolutionize the way we store and transfer data, and it is already being used in many industries, including finance, healthcare, and digital identity. Blockchain technology can be used to create secure, transparent, and efficient financial and data sharing networks, which can be used to reduce risk, improve efficiency, and reduce costs. It can also be used to create secure digital identities, which can be used to verify the identity of individuals online and to prevent fraud.

Blockchain technology is a distributed ledger technology that allows for the secure and transparent transfer of data, assets, and information. It is a decentralized, distributed and public digital ledger that is used to record transactions across many computers so that the record cannot be altered retroactively without the alteration of all subsequent blocks. This technology uses cryptography to ensure secure and immutable transactions. It is an open, distributed ledger that can record transactions between two parties efficiently and in a verifiable and permanent way. It is a system by which digital information is distributed but not copied, allowing digital assets to be securely and seamlessly transferred. The technology has the potential to revolutionize the way businesses, governments, and organizations operate and interact.

Recommender System :

A recommender system is a computer algorithm that produces personalized recommendations for users based on their preferences and past interactions. It is used in various applications such as online shopping, media streaming, and social media. The aim of a recommender system is to filter out irrelevant or less relevant items and provide users with the most suitable items for their particular situation. It does this by analysing user behaviour data and using machine learning techniques to identify patterns in that data. The system then uses these patterns to recommend items that the user is likely to be interested in.

A Recommender System is a type of information filtering system that is used to predict the likelihood of a user's preference for a certain item. It is based on user behavior and item characteristics. Recommender systems are used in a variety of applications including movies, books, music, news, restaurants, marketing, social media, etc. They provide personalized recommendations to users by learning their interests and suggesting items that they may be interested in.

A Recommender System is a system that is used to generate personalized recommendations for users. It uses algorithms to analyze user data and determine what items a user is likely to be interested in. This data can come from a variety of sources, such as past purchase history, user ratings, and demographic information. The goal of a Recommender System is to produce recommendations that are tailored to each individual user, based on their individual preferences and interests.

A Recommender System is a software application that takes data from a user and uses it to generate personalized recommendations for products, services, or other content. It uses algorithms to make predictions about a user's interests based on their past behavior and other data sources. The goal of a Recommender System is to provide the most relevant recommendations to the user, in order to increase the user's engagement with the product or service.

Smart Logistics and Supply Chain :

Smart logistics and supply chain management are the new trends in the industry, which have been enabled by the introduction of digital technology. Smart logistics and supply chain management focuses on the use of advanced technologies such as artificial intelligence, data analytics,

Internet of Things (IoT), machine learning, and predictive analytics to improve the efficiency of logistics and supply chain operations. Smart logistics and supply chain management provide a more transparent and efficient way to track goods, optimize inventory levels, reduce delivery costs, and improve overall customer experience. This technology also helps companies to optimize their operations and improve their overall profitability.

Smart logistics and supply chain are a form of supply chain management that uses the internet of things (IoT), artificial intelligence (AI), and other cutting-edge technologies to improve efficiency, speed, and accuracy of the supply chain process. By using technology to monitor and track goods in the supply chain, companies can better manage inventory, reduce costs, and increase customer satisfaction. Smart logistics and supply chain can also help companies make better decisions about their strategies, operations, and supply chain partners. This technology can also help companies better understand their customers and their needs, allowing them to tailor their services to meet those needs.

Smart logistics and supply chain is an approach to supply chain management that utilizes data analytics, artificial intelligence, machine learning, and other digital technologies to optimize the movement of goods from source to customer. This approach can help reduce costs, improve efficiency, and increase customer satisfaction. Smart logistics and supply chain management can help companies to better monitor the movement of goods, predict delays or supply chain problems, and adjust quickly to changing customer needs. It can also help with inventory management, providing real-time information about stock levels, costs, and trends. Smart logistics and supply chain management can provide valuable insights into customer behavior and preferences and help companies to better understand their target markets.

Smart logistics and supply chain are logistics and supply chain systems that use the latest in technology and automation to improve efficiency and accuracy. This includes the use of sensors and artificial intelligence to track and manage inventory, as well as predictive analytics and forecasting to anticipate customer demand. Smart logistics and supply chains are also designed to improve communication between stakeholders, such as customers, suppliers, and manufacturers. This can help reduce costs and maximize efficiency.

Industrial Automation and Control :

Industrial automation and control is the use of computers and other automated systems to control and monitor the operations of industrial processes. Automation and control systems are used in many industries, including manufacturing, energy, aerospace, automotive, and healthcare. Automation and control systems can be used to automate production processes, monitor safety and environmental conditions, and optimize the efficiency of production operations. Automation and control systems are used to reduce costs and improve quality, while providing better control and visibility over production processes. Automation and control systems can also provide predictive maintenance, which can help to reduce downtime and improve overall system performance.

Industrial automation and control is the use of automated systems and software to control and monitor industrial processes, machines, and equipment. It includes a variety of technologies and systems such as programmable logic controllers (PLCs), distributed control systems (DCSs), and supervisory control and data acquisition (SCADA) systems. Automation and control systems are used in a wide variety of industrial applications, from manufacturing and production processes to tracking and monitoring systems. They can help increase efficiency, reduce costs, and improve safety and reliability.

This field is concerned with the design and implementation of automated systems that allow for the control of industrial processes. It involves the use of computer-based systems, robots, and other automated technologies to help improve the efficiency and safety of industrial operations. The goal of industrial automation and control is to maximize productivity and minimize costs while ensuring that safety regulations are followed. Industrial automation and control is used in a wide range of industries, including manufacturing, automotive, aerospace, healthcare, and energy. This field is also increasingly being utilized in the development of smart cities, wherein the use of automated systems helps to better manage traffic, energy consumption, and other city-wide resources.

Industrial automation and control is the use of control systems, such as computers or robots, to operate and manage industrial machinery, processes, and infrastructures. Industrial automation and control systems are used to improve efficiency, accuracy, and safety in the industrial production process. Automation and control can be used for everything from regulating the temperature in a factory, to controlling the speed of a conveyor belt, to monitoring the production of a product. Automation and control systems can be programmed to respond to changes in a production environment, allowing for less human intervention and increased accuracy. Automation and control systems can also be used to monitor, analyze, and diagnose problems in the production process, helping to ensure a higher quality product.

Edge Computing :

Edge computing is the practice of processing data near the source of the data, instead of sending all of the data to a data center or cloud for processing. This is done to reduce latency, bandwidth requirements, and cost associated with communication between the source and the data center. Edge computing is used in various applications such as industrial automation, autonomous vehicles, connected home IoT devices, and smart cities.

Edge computing is a distributed computing paradigm that brings computation and data storage closer to the location where it is needed, to improve response times and save bandwidth. It is used in IoT applications to process data from devices such as sensors and cameras, and can be used to optimise the data processing flow between devices, networks and cloud. Edge computing provides a way to process data more quickly and securely, as data is processed closer to the source, reducing latency and enabling real-time decision-making. Edge computing also reduces the amount of data that needs to be sent to the cloud, reducing data transfer costs, and ensuring that data is secure and not exposed to the internet.

Edge Computing is a distributed computing paradigm in which computation and data storage are performed at the edge of the network, near the source of the data. It brings the ability to process data closer to where it is being generated, as opposed to sending it over the network to a centralised data centre or cloud. This reduces latency, increases security, and can reduce the amount of data that needs to be transmitted over the network. Edge computing can be used in many different applications, from industrial IoT and automation, to autonomous vehicles and smart cities.

Edge computing is a distributed computing system that enables the processing of data closer to the source or the edge of the network. It is a method of computing that brings computation and data storage closer to the devices and users that generate and utilize the data. Edge computing generally operates on devices such as routers, switches, gateways, and endpoints located at the edge of the network, rather than in a central location. This architecture helps to reduce latency, lower bandwidth requirements and improve response times. Edge computing is especially beneficial in areas where there is limited or no access to the cloud, or where real-time processing is required. It can also help to reduce costs associated with storage and bandwidth by enabling local storage and processing.

3D-Bioprinting :

3D-bioprinting is a kind of 3D printing technology used to manufacture biological materials, such as human tissue and organs. This technology is based on the principles of additive manufacturing, which involves building objects layer by layer. The process involves the use of computer-aided design (CAD) software to create a 3D model of the desired object. The 3D model is then sent to a 3D bioprinter, which uses specialized materials and techniques to create the object. The materials used in 3D bioprinting include biological cells, biological materials, and biomaterials. The cells and materials used may come from either the patient or a donor. The 3D bioprinter then precisely places the cells and materials layer by layer to form the desired object.

The potential applications of 3D bioprinting are immense. This technology could be used to create organs and tissues for organ transplants, to repair damaged tissues or organs, and to create artificial organs for drug testing and other purposes. Additionally, 3D bioprinting could potentially be used to create personalized medical treatments and to advance research in the field of regenerative medicine.

Reinforcement Learning

Reinforcement Learning :

Reinforcement learning is an area of artificial intelligence that focuses on finding optimal strategies for an agent to use in order to maximize a long-term reward. Reinforcement Learning algorithms learn from the environment by trial and error, so they can identify the most beneficial actions to take in order to reach the desired outcome. It is often used to teach robots to complete tasks, play games, and other applications.

Reinforcement Learning is a type of Machine Learning algorithm that allows software agents to learn from their environment through trial and error. The goal is to maximize some measure of cumulative reward by taking actions in the environment. Through a process known as Q-learning, the agent learns to make a certain set of decisions in order to maximize reward. This type of learning has been used in robotics, video games, and other AI applications.

Reinforcement learning is a type of machine learning algorithm that allows an agent to learn how to behave in an environment by performing actions and seeing the results. It is often used in robotics, control, optimization, and other complex decision-making tasks. The goal of reinforcement learning is to learn a policy that maximizes a numerical reward signal. The agent interacts with the environment by performing actions and observing the reward signal. It then updates its internal values, or policies, to maximize the expected reward signal over time.

Reinforcement Learning is a type of machine learning that focuses on learning from actions taken in an environment by trial and error and rewards or punishment, rather than from explicit instructions. It involves using a set of algorithms to enable an agent (a computer system, robot, etc.) to interact with an environment and learn how to achieve a desired outcome based on feedback from the environment. The agent can learn from its mistakes and form strategies to maximize its reward over time.

Reinforcement Learning is a branch of Artificial Intelligence (AI) that focuses on how software agents should take actions in an environment to maximize a cumulative reward. It is an area of machine learning inspired by behaviorist psychology, concerned with how software agents ought to take actions in an environment so as to maximize some notion of cumulative reward.

Reinforcement Learning is used in many different types of applications, including robotics, game playing, industrial control, and natural language processing. It is particularly useful for solving problems that are too complex for traditional AI approaches. It has recently seen a resurgence in popularity due to advances in deep learning. By combining deep learning with reinforcement learning, powerful agents can be created that can learn to play complex games and perform sophisticated tasks.

Knowledge Representation and Reasoning :

Knowledge representation and reasoning (KRR) is the process of representing knowledge in a way that makes it easier for computers to understand and use. KRR technologies enable machines to understand and reason about the environment in which they are operating, as well as provide an understanding of the behavior and relationships between objects, events, and situations.

Knowledge Representation and Reasoning (KRR) is the field of artificial intelligence that deals with how to represent information and how to use it to make decisions. KRR is concerned with the development of methods and techniques that enable computers to represent and reason with knowledge and data. This includes the development of ontologies, logic and various other formalisms. KRR is used to enable computers to reason with facts, rules and other forms of knowledge. It is essential for the development of intelligent systems, such as expert systems and robotics.

Knowledge Representation and Reasoning (KRR) is a subfield of Artificial Intelligence that deals with representing knowledge in a form that can be used by machines to reason and draw conclusions. KRR is concerned with representing knowledge in a form that can be used by machines to draw conclusions, solve problems, and make decisions. It involves the use of a variety of techniques, such as logic, probability, fuzzy logic, and Bayesian networks. KRR lies at the intersection of several different fields, including mathematics, computer science, and psychology. KRR systems are used in many different applications, including natural language processing, robotics, medical diagnosis, and financial analysis.

KRR technologies provide a common language for computers to communicate with each other and with humans. They enable machines to learn and provide meaningful insights from data. KRR can be used to develop intelligent systems that can make decisions and solve problems. KRR technologies are used in many areas of AI, including natural language processing, robotics, and machine learning.

Knowledge Representation and Reasoning (KRR) is a subfield of Artificial Intelligence (AI) that focuses on representing knowledge about the world in a way that a computer can understand and use to solve problems and reason about the environment. It is the process of representing knowledge in a structured form, such as a logical language or a graphical model, so that it can be used by a computer to solve problems. KRR is important because it allows computers to make decisions and take actions based on the knowledge they have acquired. This is used in robotics, natural language processing, expert systems, and other AI applications. KRR algorithms allow computers to process information, draw logical conclusions, and reason with facts, even when the data is incomplete or uncertain.

Planning and Scheduling :

Planning and scheduling are important tools for businesses of any size. Planning involves setting goals and objectives and creating a strategy for achieving them. Scheduling involves organizing activities and tasks to ensure they are completed in an efficient and timely manner. Planning and scheduling can help reduce costs, improve efficiency, and increase productivity. They can also help to ensure that goals are met on time and within budget. Planning and scheduling can help businesses stay organized and focused on their goals, providing the structure and discipline necessary to succeed.

Planning and scheduling are essential components of project management. Planning involves setting objectives and determining the best course of action to achieve them. Scheduling involves allocating time, resources, and personnel to implement the plan. Planning and scheduling are important for ensuring a project is completed on time and within budget. Proper planning and scheduling will also help to reduce risks, increase efficiency, and maximize the effectiveness of the project.

The use of AI in planning and scheduling is becoming increasingly popular in the industrial and business sectors. AI can help plan and schedule tasks in a more efficient and cost-effective manner than manual methods. AI-based planning and scheduling systems can also take into account various variables such as weather, customer preferences, and other external factors to optimize the plans and schedules. AI can also be used to automate the process of creating and changing plans and schedules. This can save time and reduce costs associated with manual planning and scheduling. AI-based planning and scheduling systems can also be used to monitor and adjust plans and schedules in real-time to ensure they are optimized.

Planning and scheduling in Artificial Intelligence (AI) is an area of computer science that seeks to create a machine-based system that can automatically make decisions and create plans for a given set of conditions. Planning and scheduling in AI is a complex field of research and has been the subject of extensive research for decades. It is a key area in the development of autonomous systems, and has been used in many applications such as robotics, manufacturing, logistics, and navigation. The goal of planning and scheduling in AI is to create an intelligent agent that can make decisions based on a given set of conditions and parameters, and then execute the decisions in an efficient and consistent manner. This involves a range of techniques and algorithms, such as heuristics, search algorithms, constraint satisfaction, and temporal reasoning. By combining the various techniques, it is possible to create complex planning and scheduling systems that can handle complex tasks.

Planning and Scheduling in AI is the process of creating, maintaining, and executing efficient plans and schedules to achieve the goals of an AI system. This involves making decisions about what tasks need to be accomplished, when they should be completed, and how to best allocate resources to ensure the successful completion of the tasks. AI planning and scheduling algorithms are used to identify the most efficient sequence of actions to achieve a given goal, as well as identify potential conflicts and generate schedules that minimize the risk of these conflicts occurring. By leveraging AI to optimize planning and scheduling decisions, organizations can reduce costs, increase efficiency, and improve customer service.

Knowledge Discovery and Data Mining :

Knowledge discovery and data mining in AI are the process of uncovering patterns and trends in large datasets that can be used to make predictions and decisions. The process involves using algorithms and other techniques to determine relationships and patterns in large amounts of data. This enables computers to make more informed decisions and predictions from the data. The ultimate goal of knowledge discovery and data mining is to enable computers to provide more accurate and insightful information for decision-making.

Knowledge Discovery and Data Mining (KDD) is a process of extracting meaningful information from large datasets. It is a subfield of Artificial Intelligence (AI) that focuses on creating models and algorithms to uncover patterns and relationships from large datasets. KDD involves the application of data mining, machine learning, statistics, and database technologies to analyze data. It is used to discover patterns, correlations, and trends in large datasets, and to generate insights that can be used to make informed decisions. KDD is an important part of AI, and is used in many areas such as healthcare, finance, and marketing. KDD has applications in a variety of domains, including business intelligence, customer relationship management, healthcare, and predictive analytics.

The process of knowledge discovery and data mining in AI is the process of uncovering patterns and trends in large datasets to provide insight for decision-making. This process involves collecting, cleaning, and analyzing data to uncover previously unknown relationships and insights. AI-based data mining and knowledge discovery techniques can help businesses make better decisions by uncovering hidden patterns and relationships in data. AI-based data mining and knowledge discovery techniques can be used to find patterns in customer behavior, understand customer preferences, detect fraud and anomalies, predict future trends, and much more.

Biometrics :

Biometrics in AI is the use of biometric data to develop and improve artificial intelligence (AI) systems. Biometric data can include facial recognition, voice recognition, fingerprint recognition, and other forms of biological data. AI systems can use biometric data to improve accuracy and reduce errors in a variety of tasks, such as authentication, identity verification, and fraud detection. AI systems can also use biometric data to determine individual preferences and patterns of behavior, allowing companies to better target their marketing and advertising efforts. In addition, AI systems can use biometric data to personalize services, such as healthcare and education, to meet the needs of individuals more effectively.

Biometrics in AI is the use of biological data such as fingerprints, facial recognition, and voice recognition to authenticate people, identify individuals, and provide enhanced security. AI-driven biometrics can be used to protect financial accounts, secure online transactions and physical access control, and even to detect fraud. By using biometrics, organizations can minimize the risk of unauthorized access and provide a secure and convenient way to authenticate users. AI-powered biometrics can also help to identify people in large crowds, and can be used to detect certain behaviors or patterns in a person's interactions with a system.

Biometrics in AI refers to the use of biometric data to identify, recognize, and authenticate people or objects. It is an emerging field of technology that is being used more and more in various applications. Biometrics in AI can be used to provide secure access to physical and digital spaces, help detect and prevent fraud, and even identify and track people in real-time. This technology can be used in a variety of ways, including facial recognition, fingerprint recognition, voice recognition, and even iris recognition. Biometrics in AI can be used to help automate tasks and improve accuracy, efficiency, and security of data.

Virtual Agents :

Virtual agents in AI are computer programs or software applications that mimic human conversation and behavior in order to interact with users via natural language processing and dialogue systems. They are designed to simulate the conversation of a human being and interact with users in a conversational way. Typical applications include customer service, automated help desks, and virtual assistants. Virtual agents can be used to answer customer service questions, provide product advice, guide users through processes, and provide personalized experiences.

Virtual agents in artificial intelligence (AI) are computer programs that can interact with users and simulate the behaviors of human beings. Virtual agents usually provide automated customer service, such as answering questions, providing product information, and helping customers make purchases. They are powered by natural language processing, machine learning, and other AI technologies. Virtual agents are becoming increasingly popular in customer service, as they can provide more accurate and personalized responses to customer inquiries.

Virtual agents in AI are software programs that simulate conversations with humans. They are used to provide customer service, automate tasks, and complete transactions. These agents are powered by natural language processing (NLP) and machine learning (ML) technologies. AI-based virtual agents are able to understand a user's intent and provide relevant answers. They can also be used to automate processes and complete transactions.

Autonomous Agents :

Autonomous agents in AI are software agents that can autonomously act on their environment and make decisions without any human intervention. The goal of such agents is to use artificial intelligence to enable them to perceive their environment, reason about it, and take action in order to pursue their goals. Autonomous agents can be used in a variety of applications, from robotics to natural language processing.

Autonomous agents in AI are intelligent agents that can act independently in an environment and make decisions based on their environment, goals, and beliefs. Autonomous agents are used for a variety of tasks, from providing medical advice and recommendations to providing search results and recommendations for online shopping. Autonomous agents are typically designed to act in an environment with multiple agents, where the agents interact with each other through communication protocols. The autonomous agents can use techniques such as machine learning, natural language processing, and game theory to make decisions and interact with other agents.

Autonomous agents are computer programs that are designed to act independently of human intervention. They are programmed to act in the environment, perform certain tasks and make decisions without any external input. Autonomous agents are used in Artificial Intelligence (AI) applications such as robotics, machine learning, natural language processing, and expert systems. Autonomous agents are used to automate complex tasks, analyze data and make decisions based on the data they receive. They can be used to develop more efficient and effective systems and processes. Autonomous agents can also be used to identify patterns that can be used to make predictions and recommendations.

Autonomous Vehicles :

Autonomous vehicles (AVs) are vehicles that are capable of sensing their environment and navigating without human input. They are powered by artificial intelligence (AI) technologies, such as machine learning, computer vision, and natural language processing. Autonomous vehicles have the potential to revolutionize transportation by providing a safe, efficient, and cost-effective way to move people and goods. Autonomous vehicles are already being tested on public roads around the world, and they are expected to become mainstream in the near future.

Autonomous vehicles use artificial intelligence (AI) to autonomously navigate roads and highways. AI technology is used to enable the vehicles to perceive their environment and make decisions, such as when to turn, accelerate, decelerate, and stop. AI technologies used in autonomous vehicles include computer vision, machine learning, deep learning, natural language processing, and more. Autonomous vehicles use these technologies to safely and efficiently navigate roads and highways, while reducing the risk of human error.

Autonomous vehicles are a form of artificial intelligence (AI) technology that enables a vehicle to operate without human input. Autonomous vehicles are equipped with sensors, cameras, and AI algorithms that enable them to recognize their environment and make decisions in real time. Autonomous vehicles have the potential to significantly reduce traffic fatalities and improve the safety of roads and highways, as well as reduce fuel consumption and air pollution. Autonomous vehicles can also improve the efficiency of traffic flow, and reduce the need for parking spaces. Autonomous vehicles can also revolutionize the transportation industry, allowing for the delivery of goods and services in a more efficient and cost-effective manner.

Affective Computing :

Affective computing is a branch of artificial intelligence (AI) that focuses on understanding and responding to the emotions of humans. It is the development of systems and applications that can recognize, interpret, process, and simulate human emotions and behavior. Affective computing systems are designed to respond to the emotional states of users, such as happiness, sadness, fear, or anger, and can provide feedback and guidance in real-time. Such systems can be used in a variety of applications, such as for healthcare, education, and entertainment.

Affective computing is a field of artificial intelligence (AI) research which focuses on the development of systems that can recognize, interpret, process, and simulate human emotions. This technology can be applied to a variety of applications, including virtual agents, educational technologies, health care, and interactive multimedia. Affective computing is an interdisciplinary field that integrates psychology, sociology, linguistics, and computer science, with the goal of designing systems that can interact with and respond to human emotions.

The goal of affective computing is to enable machines to recognize, interpret, and respond to human emotions in an effective, natural, and appropriate manner. This can provide a more natural and immersive user experience, which is beneficial for a variety of applications. For example, in health care, affective computing can be used to provide personalized health care services that are tailored to the emotional state of the patient. Similarly, in educational technologies, affective computing can be used to detect and respond to students' emotions in order to provide an engaging and adaptive learning experience.

Natural Language Generation :

Natural Language Generation (NLG) is a subfield of Artificial Intelligence (AI) that focuses on generating natural language text from structured data. NLG systems are able to analyze data and generate understandable human-like text that accurately reflects the underlying data. The applications of NLG range from summarizing data in reports, to providing personalized advice in customer service, to generating interactive chatbot conversations. NLG systems are capable of understanding context and conversational nuance, and can generate language that is tailored to the user's preferences.

Natural language generation (NLG) is a subfield of artificial intelligence (AI) focused on generating natural language from data. NLG systems are used to automatically generate language from structured data, such as knowledge bases, databases, and logical forms. This type of AI technology can be used to generate natural language summaries of data, generate reports, and even create entire stories from structured data. NLG can also be used in natural language processing (NLP) applications, to interpret and generate natural language for dialogue systems.

Natural Language Generation (NLG) is a branch of Artificial Intelligence which deals with the generation of natural language text from a given set of data. NLG systems analyze data, interpret it, and generate meaningful language that can be used in various applications. NLG systems are used in a variety of tasks, such as summarizing data, generating reports, providing answers to questions, and generating personalized emails and notifications. NLG systems can also be used to generate descriptions of images, videos, and sound. NLG technology is being used to improve the way businesses interact with customers, to generate automated product reviews, and to generate automated news stories.

AI Grows Up :

AI is growing up rapidly. In the past, AI was mostly used for simple tasks like playing chess or recognizing images. Now, AI is being used to solve complex problems in many industries, such as healthcare, finance, and transportation. AI systems are becoming more sophisticated and are able to think for themselves and make decisions. AI is being used to automate processes, predict outcomes, and personalize experiences. In the future, AI will continue to grow, becoming more powerful and capable of taking on more complex tasks. As AI grows up, it will become increasingly important to understand the ethical implications of AI and ensure that it is used responsibly.

AI has grown up in leaps and bounds over the past few years. AI is becoming increasingly powerful and capable, able to tackle more complex and real-world problems than ever before. We're seeing advances in everything from natural language processing and image recognition to robotics and driverless cars. AI is no longer limited to the realm of science fiction; it's becoming part of our everyday lives. AI-enabled products and services are being developed for a wide range of applications, from healthcare and finance to retail and manufacturing. AI is being used to automate mundane tasks, assist in decision-making, and improve customer experiences. As AI continues to evolve and become more powerful, we can expect to see more applications and uses for it in the near future.

AI is growing up in leaps and bounds, with new advancements and applications appearing every day. AI is being used to solve complex problems, automate tedious tasks, and provide insights that would otherwise be impossible. As AI continues to mature, it will become more capable of complex decision-making, more accurate in its predictions, and more efficient in its operations. AI is being used in a variety of industries, from healthcare to finance, and from retail to manufacturing. AI is being used to improve customer service, create personalized experiences, and enable businesses to make data-driven decisions. AI is also being used to automate mundane tasks, reduce costs, and increase efficiency. As AI continues to grow and evolve, it will become an increasingly important part of our lives, and will reshape the way we work, live, and play.

Evolution strategies :

Evolution strategies are a class of optimization algorithms used to search for optimal parameters of a given system. They use the principles of evolutionary computing, where a population of candidate solutions is iteratively improved through selection, mutation and recombination. They are typically used to optimize complex, non-convex problems, such as finding the best parameters of a neural network, or the optimal control parameters for a robot.

Evolution strategies (ES) are a family of black-box optimization algorithms that are inspired by evolutionary biology and use evolution to optimize parameters of a system. ES algorithms are used to solve difficult optimization problems in which the objective function is unknown or too complex to calculate the derivatives of. The algorithms use a population of parameter vectors that are mutated and evaluated to generate new generations of parameter vectors with better fitting parameters. The end result is a set of parameters that optimize the system being studied.

Evolution strategies (ES) is a family of black-box optimization algorithms, inspired by evolutionary biology, used to solve difficult problems in machine learning and artificial intelligence. ES algorithms are based on the concept of natural selection and are used to optimize a given objective function over a set of parameters. They work by generating a population of candidate solutions, then iteratively selecting the best solutions and recombining them to create a new generation of solutions.

The process continues until the objective function is minimized or maximized. The resulting population is then the optimal set of parameters for the given problem. ES algorithms are robust and efficient, and have been used to optimize a wide variety of problems, including neural networks, reinforcement learning, and robotics.

Maintenance scheduling with genetic algorithms :

Genetic algorithms are a type of optimization technique used to solve complex problems. They are inspired by principles of natural selection and evolution, and can be applied to a variety of problems, including maintenance scheduling. Maintenance scheduling is the process of organizing and scheduling maintenance activities to ensure that equipment and systems are properly maintained and operated.

In maintenance scheduling with genetic algorithms, the algorithm can be used to optimize a maintenance schedule by finding an efficient solution that meets all the requirements of the maintenance schedule. The genetic algorithm works by creating a population of possible solutions and then "evolving" them over time. The algorithm evaluates each solution in the population based on a fitness function and then chooses the best solution. The fitness function takes into account factors such as cost, time, safety, and risk. The algorithm then modifies the best solution and repeats the process until an optimal solution is found.

Genetic algorithms can be used to solve complex problems in maintenance scheduling that are difficult to solve using traditional methods. This can be useful for optimizing maintenance schedules for large systems or for finding the optimal solution for a variety of maintenance tasks. Furthermore, genetic algorithms can help to reduce costs and improve the efficiency of a maintenance schedule.

Genetic algorithms:

Genetic algorithms are a class of algorithms that are inspired by the process of natural selection. They are used for solving optimization and search problems and are based on the idea of survival of the fittest. Genetic algorithms use a process of selection and recombination to generate new solutions from existing solutions. The new solutions are evaluated and the best are selected for further recombination. This process is repeated until a satisfactory solution is found. Genetic algorithms are often used in machine learning, robotics, and other areas of artificial intelligence.

Genetic algorithms are optimization algorithms that use evolutionary principles such as natural selection, mutation, and crossover to solve complex problems. The algorithm begins by randomly generating a population of solutions, then evaluates each solution based on a given set of parameters or "fitness" criteria. The best solutions are then selected and combined to produce a new, better solution, and the process is repeated until an optimal solution is found. Genetic algorithms have been used to solve a variety of problems, including optimization of complex systems, scheduling, and pattern recognition

Genetic algorithms are a type of artificial intelligence that use principles of natural selection and genetics to solve problems and find solutions. They are based on the idea of evolution and the notion that the fittest solutions will survive and be passed on to the next generation. Genetic algorithms work by creating a population of solutions and then applying various selection and mutation techniques to optimize the solutions and find the best one. The solutions are tested and the fittest ones are selected and then mutated. This process is repeated until the best solution is found. Genetic algorithms can be used to solve a wide variety of problems, from scheduling to routing and optimization.

Simulation of natural evolution :

Simulation of natural evolution is a type of computer simulation used to study the process of natural selection and evolutionary change in populations of organisms. It can be used to test hypotheses about the mechanisms of evolution, to explore the patterns of evolutionary change, and to gain insights into the dynamics of natural selection. The simulation usually involves a population of virtual organisms, which are subject to various environmental conditions and/or genetic changes. These organisms compete for resources and reproduce, with the fittest individuals surviving to pass on their traits to the next generation. Over time, the population evolves in response to the conditions of the environment and the genetic changes of the population.

Simulation of natural evolution is a type of computer simulation that models the process of natural selection and evolution. These simulations are used to study evolutionary dynamics and to model the emergence of complex traits and behaviors.

By simulating the environment, the conditions in which organisms live, and the genetic and environmental factors that influence the selection and reproduction of individuals, these simulations can help scientists better understand the evolution of species. These simulations can also help identify possible evolutionary pathways and uncover trends and patterns in the data. The simulation of natural evolution can also be used to create virtual worlds of virtual species, allowing scientists to explore how these species might interact and evolve in a similar way to their real counterparts.

Simulations of natural evolution can be used to explore a wide range of evolutionary processes and phenomena. Simulations can be used to explore the effects of selection, mutation, genetic drift, and other evolutionary forces on populations. Simulations can also be used to test hypotheses about the dynamics of populations and the impact of different evolutionary strategies and conditions.

Simulations can be used to explore the genetic and phenotypic consequences of different mating systems, including sexual selection and inbreeding. Simulations can be used to explore the emergence of novel traits, the effects of different environmental conditions, and the impacts of colonization and migration on populations. Finally, simulations can be used to explore the interplay between ecological and evolutionary processes, helping us to better understand how species and populations interact with each other and their environment.

Evolutionary computation :

Evolutionary computation is a type of artificial intelligence (AI) that uses algorithms inspired by the process of natural selection to find solutions to optimization and search problems. It uses computer-generated solutions to problems that would be difficult or impossible to solve using traditional methods. This type of AI typically involves the generation of multiple possible solutions, with the best solutions being selected and improved upon for the next generation. This process is repeated until an optimal solution is found. Evolutionary computation has been applied to a variety of problem domains, including robotics, machine learning, game theory, and bioinformatics.

Evolutionary computation is a subset of artificial intelligence algorithms that use evolutionary principles such as natural selection, mutation, and recombination to search for solutions to difficult problems. Evolutionary algorithms are used to solve difficult optimization problems, such as finding the shortest path through a maze or the most efficient design for a bridge. Evolutionary computing is also used for discovering new drugs, creating new materials, and designing robots. Evolutionary computation is based on the idea that a population of solutions can evolve and develop over time, and that the best solutions can be found by simulating the natural selection process.

Evolutionary computation is an artificial intelligence technique that uses evolutionary algorithms to solve complex optimization problems. It is based on the principles of natural selection and the process of evolution in the biological world. Evolutionary computation typically involves the creation of an initial population of randomly generated solutions to a given problem, and then refining these solutions over time through a process of selection, mutation, and crossover. The resulting solutions are known as "evolved" solutions, and are typically far more efficient than those generated through traditional artificial intelligence methods. Evolutionary computation has been applied to solve a variety of problems, including robotics, scheduling, image recognition, and machine learning.

Competitive learning :

Competitive learning is an artificial neural network learning algorithm in which nodes compete for the right to respond to a subset of the input data. It is a type of unsupervised learning in which nodes compete for the right to be activated by input from the environment. The nodes with the strongest response to the input data are determined and then used to generate a response. It is most commonly used in pattern recognition and classification applications.

Competitive learning is a type of unsupervised learning algorithm in which neurons in a neural network compete to be the first to respond correctly to a given input. In the process of competition, each neuron becomes specialized to recognize a particular input pattern or class of patterns. The idea of competitive learning was first introduced by Teuvo Kohonen in 1982.

Competitive learning algorithms work by having a set of neurons compete for the right to respond to a given input. Each neuron takes the input, processes it, and then produces an output. The neuron with the highest output wins the competition, and its output is used as the response to the input. The other neurons in the network learn from this result and modify their weights to increase their chances of winning the next competition. By repeating this process, the neurons become specialized in recognizing particular input patterns.

Self-organising neural networks :

Self-organising neural networks are artificial neural networks that can adjust their connections and structures autonomously. They are able to learn from the data they receive and adjust their structure accordingly. This type of neural network is useful for tasks such as clustering and classification. They are also used in robotics and machine learning applications.

Self-organising neural networks are a type of artificial neural network which are capable of learning by themselves. They have the ability to modify their weights and structure based on the data they are presented with. This type of network is useful for applications such as clustering, pattern recognition and classification. Unlike other neural networks, self-organising neural networks do not require extensive training and are able to learn by themselves, making them very efficient and powerful.

Self-organising neural networks are artificial neural networks that are capable of autonomously learning and adapting to changing inputs. They are trained using unsupervised learning algorithms, which means they learn without being told what to do. Self-organising neural networks are often used for pattern recognition, image recognition, and object recognition applications. They are also used in reinforcement learning and are capable of learning from mistakes made in the past and improving upon them.

Bidirectional associative memory :

Bidirectional associative memory (BAM) is an artificial neural network model used to store and recall patterns. It is an associative memory, meaning that it can recall patterns based on incomplete information. The BAM is composed of two layers, an input layer and an output layer. The network is trained by presenting input patterns to the input layer and output patterns to the output layer. The input and output layers are connected by weights, and the network learns by adjusting the weights between the two layers. The network can recall patterns by presenting an incomplete input pattern to the input layer and retrieving the associated output pattern from the output layer.

Bidirectional associative memory (BAM) is a type of artificial neural network that enables the storage and recall of memories in both directions. It is a type of auto-associative neural network in which the same set of weights and activation functions are used for both the forward and backward passes. This allows the network to store and recall memories in both directions—from inputs to outputs and vice versa. BAM networks are used for a variety of applications, including pattern recognition, classification, and natural language processing.

Bidirectional associative memory (BAM) is a type of artificial neural network that stores and retrieves information in both directions. It is a type of associative memory, which means it can store and recall pairs of associated information. BAMs are used for a variety of tasks, including pattern recognition, classification, and clustering. BAMs are a type of recurrent neural network (RNN) that can store patterns in both directions. This allows the model to learn associations between inputs and outputs, and can be used to recognize patterns and classify data. BAMs have been used in a variety of domains, such as natural language processing, image recognition, and speech recognition.

The Hopfield network :

The Hopfield network is a type of artificial neural network developed by John Hopfield in 1982. It is a recurrent neural network that is used for associative memory and optimization. The Hopfield network is composed of neurons or nodes, which are connected to each other by weighted connections or edges. The weights of the connections are adjusted to store a set of patterns in the neurons. The network can then be used to recall one of the stored patterns in response to an input pattern. The Hopfield network is a type of energy-based model and can be used to solve a variety of optimization problems.

The Hopfield network is an artificial neural network developed by John Hopfield in 1982. It is a type of recurrent neural network (RNN) and is based on the Hebbian learning rule. The Hopfield network has the ability to store a large number of patterns in its memory, by associating them with the states of neurons in the network. When presented with a new pattern, it can recall the closest stored pattern from its memory. It is useful for solving optimization problems, such as the traveling salesman problem.

The Hopfield network is a type of recurrent artificial neural network used for pattern recognition and optimization. It was developed by John Hopfield in 1982 and is based on the concept of energy minimization. The network is composed of a set of neurons, each neuron representing a single binary value (0 or 1).

The neurons are connected with each other via weighted connections. The weights of the connections are calculated according to the connection's input value, which is determined by the data set that the network is trying to learn. The network is trained by adjusting the weights of the connections so that the energy of the system is minimized. Once the training is complete, the network can be used to recognize patterns or to solve optimization problems.

The Hopfield network is a type of artificial neural network that is used to store and recall patterns. It is based on associative memory, which is a type of memory that stores information by associating patterns of activity between neurons. The Hopfield network is composed of neurons that are connected to each other in a fully-connected, symmetric pattern.

Each neuron is associated with one bit of information, and the network can be used to store and recall patterns of multiple bits. The network is trained by presenting it with a set of patterns, which are encoded as the activity of the neurons in the network. The patterns are then stored in the connections between the neurons. When a new pattern is presented to the network, it is compared to the stored patterns and the closest match is recalled. This allows the network to recognize and recall patterns even if they are slightly different than the stored patterns.

Multilayer neural networks :

Multilayer neural networks are a type of artificial neural network that consists of multiple layers of neurons, or nodes. These networks use a supervised learning approach, in which the output of the network is compared against labeled data to adjust the weights of the neurons in each layer. This process is repeated until the network converges on a set of weights that provide the desired output. Multilayer neural networks can be used for a variety of tasks, such as image classification, natural language processing, and time series analysis.

Multilayer neural networks are artificial neural networks that contain more than one layer of neurons. These networks are used to solve complex problems such as pattern recognition and classification. They have an input layer, one or more hidden layers and an output layer. The input layer takes in the input data, the hidden layer processes the data, and the output layer produces the output. The hidden layers can contain various types of neurons, such as sigmoid neurons, rectified linear neurons or radial basis function neurons. Multilayer neural networks can be trained using backpropagation and other algorithms.

Multilayer neural networks are artificial neural networks that contain multiple layers of neurons. They are used in a variety of applications, such as image recognition, natural language processing, and machine learning. The layers of neurons are connected to each other and pass signals from one layer to the next. The layers are composed of neurons that have weights and biases that can be adjusted to optimize the network's performance. The weights and biases are adjusted based on the data being used and the desired outcome. Multilayer neural networks are powerful tools for analyzing complex data and making predictions.

Interaction of frames and rules :

The interaction between frames and rules is an important part of many AI systems. Frames are used to provide a structured representation of a problem domain, while rules are used to define the behavior of the system within that domain. Together, frames and rules are used to create a system that can reason about the problem domain and make decisions about it.

Frames are used to represent the objects and concepts in the problem domain and their relationships. Rules are then used to define how those objects and concepts interact with each other and how the system should respond to certain situations. For example, a rule might state that if an object A is in a certain location, then an object B should be moved to a location close by.

The interaction between frames and rules helps to create a logical and consistent system that can reason about the problem domain and make decisions. By using frames to represent the objects and concepts in the problem domain, a system can understand the relationships between them and determine the best course of action for any given situation.

Comparison of Bayesian reasoning and certainty factors :

Bayesian reasoning and certainty factors are two methods of reasoning and decision making. Bayesian reasoning is a type of probabilistic reasoning that uses Bayes' theorem to update beliefs as new evidence is observed. Certainty factors are a type of fuzzy logic that assigns weights to different pieces of evidence, allowing for more nuanced decision making than simple yes/no answers.

The primary difference between these two methods is that Bayesian reasoning is probabilistic, while certainty factors are fuzzy. Bayesian reasoning produces probabilities that represent the likelihood of a certain outcome, while certainty factors produce values that represent confidence in the accuracy of a belief. In addition, Bayesian reasoning is focused on updating beliefs as new evidence is observed, while certainty factors are focused on assigning weights to different pieces of evidence.

Bayesian reasoning is a probabilistic approach that uses prior information to calculate the probability of a certain outcome. It is based on Bayes' theorem, which states that the probability of an event is equal to the prior probability multiplied by the likelihood of that event. This approach allows for the possibility of false positives or false negatives, as the probability of an event is never certain.

Conflict resolution :

Conflict resolution is the process of resolving a dispute or conflict by finding a solution that satisfies both parties involved. It is a necessary skill for any healthy relationship, whether it be between coworkers, family members, or friends. There are various techniques for resolving conflicts such as active listening, compromise, problem-solving, and negotiation. Each technique has its own advantages and disadvantages, so choosing the best option depends on the particular situation. Ultimately, the goal of conflict resolution is to reach an agreement that both parties find acceptable.

Conflict resolution is the process of resolving a dispute or a conflict by meeting at least some of each side's needs and addressing their interests. It is an approach to discipline that focuses on problem-solving and negotiation rather than relying solely on punishment. Strategies used to resolve conflict may include negotiation, mediation, arbitration, collaborative problem solving, and other forms of alternative dispute resolution.

Conflict resolution is the process of resolving a dispute or a conflict by meeting at least some of each side's needs and addressing their interests. It is a process of identifying and addressing the underlying concerns that are causing the conflict, and finding a solution that all parties involved can accept. It involves understanding the source of the conflict, exploring possible solutions, and ultimately negotiating a resolution that is agreeable to all parties. Conflict resolution can be achieved through mediation, negotiation, arbitration, or other methods.

Mediation :

Mediation in AI is the use of AI technology to assist in the resolution of disputes between two or more parties. It involves the use of algorithms, machine learning, natural language processing, and other AI techniques to analyze data and facilitate the resolution of disputes. AI mediation can reduce the time and cost associated with dispute resolution by automating the process and providing an impartial, unbiased approach to resolving the dispute. AI mediation can be used to help resolve a variety of disputes, from financial disputes to family disputes and more. AI mediation can provide a faster, more efficient, and more cost-effective way of resolving disputes.

Mediation in AI is the process of resolving conflicts and seeking mutually beneficial solutions between two or more entities. It involves both understanding the underlying issues and seeking a resolution that meets the needs of all parties. In AI, mediation is used to resolve disagreements between different algorithms or agents, or between humans and AI systems. It can also be used to negotiate resource allocation in multi-agent systems.

Causal Inference and Learning :

Causal inference and learning is the process of inferring causal relationships between different variables, such as predictors and outcomes, in a given data set. It involves the use of data analysis methods such as regression and machine learning algorithms to identify and explain the relationships between variables. By understanding causal relationships, researchers can make more accurate predictions and improve decision-making. Causal learning can be used to discover new insights and uncover hidden patterns in data that would otherwise remain hidden.

Causal inference and learning refers to the techniques used to infer the causal relationships between different variables in a dataset or environment. These techniques are used to identify the cause-and-effect relationships between different variables and can be used to predict how changes to one variable might affect another. Causal inference and learning can be used to construct causal models that can be used for forecasting, decision making, and policy evaluation. Examples of causal inference and learning include Bayesian networks, causal inference algorithms, and structural equation modeling.

Causal inference and learning is the process of using data and statistical methods to identify and quantify the causal relationships between variables. This type of analysis is used to determine how changes in one variable will affect another and can provide insight into complex systems. It can be used to identify the causes of certain behaviors, such as why certain people are more likely to get a certain disease, or to understand the effects of certain interventions, such as the impact of a new drug on a certain condition. In addition, causal inference and learning can be used to make predictions about the future, allowing researchers to better understand how certain variables may interact in the future.

Game Playing and Search :
Game playing and search algorithms are used to solve problems in the fields of Artificial Intelligence and Computer Science. Game playing algorithms are used to determine the best moves in a given game or situation by considering the possible outcomes of various moves.

Search algorithms are used to find optimal solutions to a problem by exploring a search space of possible solutions. Both algorithms involve using heuristics to evaluate the best move or solution in a given situation.

Game playing and search are two related fields of Artificial Intelligence (AI) that aim to find the best possible solution to a problem. Games such as chess, checkers, and Go are considered to be the most difficult for computers to solve. Search algorithms are used to search for the optimal solution to a problem in a given space. These algorithms search through a space of possible solutions and evaluate each solution based on some criteria. The most common search algorithms used in game playing and search are minimax, alpha-beta pruning, and Monte Carlo tree search.

Minimax is a simple algorithm used to find the best move in a two-player game. It works by assuming that each player is trying to maximize their score, while the opponent is trying to minimize their score. The algorithm then evaluates each possible move and selects the one that leads to the best score.

Alpha-beta pruning is an extension of minimax that reduces the number of nodes that need to be searched. It works by pruning off branches of the search tree that will not lead to better results. This allows the search to focus on the most promising branches.

Game Theory :

Game theory is a branch of mathematics that studies strategic decision-making in situations where multiple players are involved. It is used to analyze how players will interact with each other given the incentives and constraints of the game, and to determine the equilibrium strategies that will maximize their payoffs. Game theory has applications in economics, political science, psychology, biology, and many other fields.

Game theory is a branch of applied mathematics that studies strategic interactions between rational decision-makers. It is an interdisciplinary field of study that combines mathematical, psychological and economic concepts. Game theory has been used in a variety of fields, including economics, politics, psychology and biology, to analyze interactions between multiple decision-makers. Game theory studies how rational decision-makers interact in strategic situations, and how their decisions affect the outcomes of the game. It is used to analyze a wide range of scenarios, from simple games of chance such as rock-paper-scissors, to complex economic models of supply and demand. Game theory has been used to analyze the behavior of markets, to understand the behavior of political actors, and to study evolutionary biology.

Learning on Graphs :

Graphs are powerful tools for representing data and learning on them. They are used in a variety of applications including natural language processing, recommender systems, and computer vision. Graphs allow for the representation of complex relationships between objects and can be used to identify patterns and predict outcomes. Graph-based learning algorithms can be used to find hidden patterns in data and to predict future behavior. Graph-based learning also has the potential to speed up traditional machine learning algorithms, as the data can often be represented more efficiently and accurately. Graph-based learning can also help to reduce the cost of training large datasets by allowing for the reuse of existing models.

Graphs are an important data structure in many fields, such as computer science and machine learning. Graphs are often used to represent relationships between different entities, such as people, places, or topics. Learning on graphs is a field of study that focuses on using machine learning algorithms to uncover patterns and insights from graph-structured data. This type of learning is useful for understanding complex networked data, such as the structure of social networks, knowledge graphs, biological networks, and more. It can help to uncover hidden relationships between entities, as well as to predict future events or behaviors. Graph-based learning algorithms can be applied to a wide variety of tasks, such as recommendation systems, fraud detection, natural language processing, and autonomous systems.

Graphs are useful data structures that can be used in machine learning. Graphs can be used to represent relationships between different entities and to capture patterns in data. Graphs are particularly useful when trying to find relationships between different entities in a large, complex data set. By modeling the data as a graph, it becomes easier to uncover hidden patterns and relationships. Graph algorithms can be used to find clusters, detect anomalies, and detect communities in a graph, as well as to find shortest paths between nodes. Graphs can also be used for supervised learning tasks such as classification and regression. Finally, graphs can be used to identify and quantify relationships between entities, making them useful for recommendation systems.

Mathematical Optimization and Statistics :

Mathematical optimization and statistics are two closely related fields that are used to analyze data and make decisions. Mathematical optimization is the process of using mathematical methods to find optimal solutions to problems. It involves formulating a problem as a mathematical model, then finding the best possible solution to that model. Statistics, on the other hand, is the science of collecting, analyzing, interpreting, and presenting data. Statistics is used to draw meaningful conclusions from data, and is often used in conjunction with optimization to make more informed decisions. Together, mathematical optimization and statistics can be used to solve complex problems and make better decisions.

Mathematical optimization and statistics are two interrelated disciplines. Optimization is the process of finding the best solution to a given problem, while statistics is the study of the probability and behavior of data. Together, these two disciplines provide powerful tools for solving problems, making decisions, and analyzing data. Optimization techniques are used to find the best solution to a given problem. This can be done by identifying the best set of parameters, or by maximizing a given objective function. Statistics, on the other hand, is used to analyze data in order to gain insight into how it is distributed and to make predictions. It can also be used to identify trends, understand correlations, and make inferences about the data. By combining the two disciplines, researchers are able to make better decisions and solve complex problems.

Mathematical optimization and statistics are two closely related fields of mathematics. Mathematical optimization focuses on finding the best possible solution to a problem, while statistics involves collecting, analyzing, and interpreting data. Both areas of mathematics use models and techniques to solve problems and make decisions. While mathematical optimization is often used to optimize business processes, statistics is used to optimize research designs, analyze data, and draw conclusions. Both fields are used extensively in the business world to make decisions, develop strategies, and increase efficiency.

Mediation :

Mediation in AI is the process of using AI-based systems to automate conflict resolution and dispute resolution. This process involves the use of algorithms, machine learning, and natural language processing to identify the root causes of disputes, analyze the data, and then recommend a resolution. AI can be used to automate negotiations, identify potential solutions, and even predict potential outcomes so that the best possible resolution can be reached. This can be used in legal, business, and interpersonal disputes.

Mediation in AI is the process of discovering conflicts between different goals and objectives, and resolving them through negotiation, arbitration or other methods. This process helps to ensure that the AI system is operating in a manner that is consistent with the intended goals and objectives. Mediation in AI can involve both algorithmic and human-driven techniques, such as negotiations between competing AI agents, arbitration between robot teams, and automated conflict resolution between different AI systems. In addition, mediation can be used to determine when AI systems should be allowed to make decisions independently, when they should be guided by human input, and when they should be shut down.

Mediation in AI is the process of using AI to form an impartial, unbiased agreement between two or more parties. This could be to solve a dispute, negotiate a contract, or even facilitate communication between two parties. AI can be used to analyze data, identify common interests and objectives, and generate solutions that are satisfactory to all parties involved. This type of mediation can be especially useful in situations where the parties involved have conflicting interests or the situation is too complex for human mediation. AI is also able to consider a large amount of data and offer options that a human mediator might not be able to think of.

Mediation in AI refers to the process of using AI to assist in resolving disputes or conflicts between two or more parties. This can involve using AI-based algorithms to analyze data from both parties to offer insights into the dispute or conflict, or employing AI-driven chatbots to facilitate communication and negotiation between the parties. AI can also be used to automate certain tasks in the mediation process, such as scheduling meetings and providing automated updates on the status of the dispute or conflict.

Negotiation :

Negotiation in AI is the study of algorithms and techniques for two or more agents to achieve an optimal outcome in a multi-party negotiation. Negotiation in AI research spans a variety of areas, including game theory, decision theory, and machine learning. AI-based negotiation systems are used to help humans negotiate in a variety of domains, from business negotiations to automated car sharing. In addition, AI-based negotiation systems are being developed as a way to automate negotiations with autonomous agents.

Negotiation in AI is the process of two or more AI agents working together to identify possible solutions to problems. This process involves identifying goals and objectives, finding possible solutions, and agreeing on a mutually beneficial outcome. Negotiation in AI is used to solve complex problems that require multiple agents to collaborate in order to achieve an outcome. It can be used in a variety of applications, such as autonomous agents negotiating deals on behalf of businesses, agents trading items in a virtual marketplace, or robots negotiating with humans.

Negotiation in AI refers to the use of AI technologies such as machine learning, natural language processing, and computer vision to help automate the process of negotiation between two or more parties. AI-enabled negotiation enables parties to reach agreements faster and more efficiently than traditional methods, as AI models can quickly analyze data, identify patterns, and suggest optimal solutions. AI-based negotiation systems are being used in a variety of applications, including contract negotiations, supply chain management, and online auctions.

Compromise :

Compromise in AI typically refers to the ethical considerations that need to be taken into account when designing and deploying AI-based systems. This includes areas such as privacy and fairness, data security and reliability, and the potential for intentional or unintentional misuse of AI systems. It is important to determine how AI systems should interact with humans and make decisions, as well as the need to ensure that AI is transparent and accountable for its decisions. Additionally, a key component of ethical AI is the need to develop systems that are reliable and trustworthy, and that are able to protect user data and privacy.

Compromise in AI typically refers to a situation in which different stakeholders have different goals and objectives for an AI system. This often involves balancing the needs of multiple parties, such as industry, governments, and the public. In these situations, compromises can be made to ensure that all parties benefit from the deployment of AI technologies. For example, a compromise could be reached between an industry and government to ensure that the industry develops AI that is safe and secure, while still allowing the government to access certain data for its own purposes. Compromise can also involve setting standards and regulations to ensure that AI is used responsibly and ethically.

Compromise in AI can refer to a number of different things. It could mean compromising on the quality of the AI, for example using a less accurate AI algorithm in order to save costs. Compromise could also refer to different stakeholders coming to an agreement on how to use the AI, such as agreeing on who will have access to the data or the algorithms that are used. Finally, compromise could also refer to AI being used to find a solution that is acceptable to everyone, such as using AI to find a way to reduce carbon emissions without drastically impacting businesses.

Compromise in AI refers to the use of AI to negotiate and reach a compromise between two or more parties. This could involve using AI to analyze data to find the best possible outcome for all parties involved, or using AI to automate the negotiation process. AI can also be used to help identify areas of compromise that may not be immediately apparent to the parties involved.

Problem solving :

Problem solving in AI involves the use of algorithms and techniques to find solutions to complex problems. AI algorithms are designed to learn from data and to identify patterns in order to make predictions and decisions. Examples of problem solving in AI include natural language processing (NLP) for understanding spoken or written language, computer vision for identifying objects in images, and robotics for navigating and performing tasks in the physical world. AI can also be used to identify correlations between events and make decisions based on this knowledge.

Problem solving in AI involves the use of algorithms and techniques to solve complex problems that are difficult or impossible for humans to solve. This includes planning, search, optimization, scheduling, uncertainty, game playing, robotics, and natural language processing. AI techniques can be used to solve problems such as route planning, scheduling, decision making, classification, prediction, and more. AI techniques are often used to optimize processes and make decisions that would be too complex or time consuming for humans to make.

Problem solving in AI is the process of using algorithms and search techniques to make decisions and solve problems. It involves using AI to analyze data, determine the best possible course of action, and then take the appropriate steps to solve the problem. AI can be used to solve problems in a variety of areas, such as healthcare, finance, robotics, and transportation. AI can also be used to optimize existing solutions or create new solutions to problems that have never been faced before.

CHAPTER FIVE

AI Revolution

AI Revolution :

The AI revolution is a term used to describe the rapid advancement of artificial intelligence technology that is occurring in the world today. AI is being used in a variety of fields, from healthcare to finance, and its potential to revolutionize how we go about our daily lives is only beginning to be realized. AI has the potential to automate mundane tasks, better diagnose and treat illnesses, and improve decision-making processes. It can also help to improve productivity, reduce costs, and increase safety. There are many different aspects of AI, from machine learning to natural language processing, and these are being explored and developed to create new opportunities for businesses and individuals alike.

The AI revolution is a term used to describe the rapid advances in artificial intelligence (AI) technology that have been taking place over the last few years. This revolution is driving a massive transformation in the way businesses and people interact with technology, as AI-powered applications and services become more prevalent in everyday life. Businesses are utilizing AI to automate tasks, improve customer service, and make decisions faster and more accurately. AI is also being used to create new products, services and business models, driving innovation and disruption across all industries. As AI technology evolves, it is becoming increasingly powerful and versatile, enabling it to take on more complex tasks and provide more sophisticated insights. The AI revolution is changing the way people work, think, and live, and is creating new opportunities for businesses and individuals alike.

The AI revolution is a term used to describe the rapid advancement of artificial intelligence (AI) technology and its impact on modern society. AI has been around for several decades, but has recently become more accessible, powerful, and pervasive. This revolution is marked by the development of new tools and applications that are changing how we interact with technology, how businesses operate, and how people live their lives. AI is being used to automate manual processes, improve decision-making, and provide predictive analytics. In addition, AI is being used to create virtual assistants, personalize customer experiences, and develop autonomous vehicles. AI technology is also being used to revolutionize healthcare, finance, security, and many other fields. As AI technology continues to develop, it will have an even greater impact on our lives and the way we do business.

AI and Society :

The impact of AI on society is often discussed in terms of its potential to automate jobs, challenge existing social structures, and create new forms of inequality. As AI continues to evolve, it is becoming increasingly embedded in our daily lives. This has implications for how we interact with each other, how our institutions operate, and how we make decisions. AI can be used to improve the efficiency of existing processes and to develop new products and services. It can also be used to analyse large datasets, identify patterns, and make predictions. AI is also being used to automate mundane tasks, such as scheduling meetings, as well as more complex activities such as decision-making. In the medical field, AI is now being applied to diagnose diseases, detect anomalies in medical images, and even provide personalized treatments. As AI continues to evolve, it is likely to become increasingly ubiquitous in our lives and will have far-reaching implications for how we live and work.

AI has significant implications for society in both positive and negative ways. On the positive side, AI can be used to improve decision-making, automate mundane tasks, and enable more efficient use of resources. AI can also be used to identify patterns in data and create predictive models that can be used to improve safety, health, and economic conditions. On the negative side, AI can be used to automate or replace human jobs, leading to job loss and economic disruption. AI can also be used to exploit vulnerable populations due to biased data or algorithms, or to invade people's privacy. AI also has implications for security, as malicious actors can use AI to develop more sophisticated attack and defense mechanisms. Therefore, the development and use of AI must be carefully managed to ensure the greatest benefit to society.

Real Life Applications of Research Areas:

1. Machine Learning: Machine learning is used for a variety of applications such as facial recognition, online fraud detection, autonomous driving, speech recognition, medical diagnosis, and more.

2. Natural Language Processing: Natural language processing can be used for automated customer service, text analysis, translation services, automated

summarization, and more.

3. Computer Vision: Computer vision is being used in retail, healthcare, robotics, security, driverless cars, and more.

4. Data Mining: Data mining is being used to detect fraud, improve customer experience, predict customer behavior, improve marketing campaigns, and more.

5. Robotics: Robotics is being used in manufacturing, healthcare, agriculture, and a range of other industries.

6. IoT: IoT is being used for predictive maintenance, smart homes, smart cities, manage energy usage, and more.

Improving Understanding of How Humans Interact with Technology :

One way to improve understanding of how humans interact with technology is to conduct research into how people interact with different types of technology. This research can be conducted through surveys, interviews, and user testing. Surveys can provide insight into how people feel about a particular technology, their comfort level with it, and what features they would like to have. Interviews can provide deeper insights into how people use technology and how it affects their everyday tasks. User testing can help to determine how easy a particular technology is to use and the overall user experience. By studying how people interact with technology, it is possible to develop better designs and experiences that are tailored to the needs of the user.

1. Developing better user interfaces: User interfaces such as those found on computers, digital devices, and websites have an immense impact on how users interact with technology. Improving the design of user interfaces can help make using technology easier, faster, and more enjoyable.

2. Researching human-computer interaction: Understanding how users interact with technology can help inform the design of better user interfaces and technology solutions. Conducting research on human-computer interaction can help identify areas for improvement, such as how users interact with voice-based systems.

3. Enhancing natural language processing: Natural language processing is a key component of how humans interact with technology. Improving the accuracy and capability of natural language processing can help make it easier for humans to communicate with technology.

4. Designing for accessibility: Designing technology solutions with accessibility in mind can help ensure that everyone is able to interact with technology. For example, making sure technology solutions are accessible to those with visual and hearing impairments can help make them more usable.

5. Incorporating AI: Incorporating artificial intelligence into technology solutions can help improve the user experience by making it easier to interact with technology. For example, AI can be used to automate some processes and provide more accurate and personalized responses to users.

The best way to improve understanding of how humans interact with technology is to observe and study people's interactions with technology. This can be done in a variety of ways, such as conducting interviews, surveys, and field studies. Interviews and surveys can provide a wealth of information about how people use and experience technology, while field studies can provide an in-depth understanding of how people interact with technology in their everyday lives.

It is also important to consider the context in which people use technology. Different people may interact with technology differently depending on their age, gender, culture, or other factors. Therefore, it is important to take into account the context in which people use technology in order to gain a better understanding of how humans interact with technology.

Finally, it is important to consider the ways in which technology is designed and how it impacts users. Understanding how technology is designed and how it affects users can provide insight into how people interact with technology and how it can be improved.